Literacy Work Stations
Making Centers Work

Debbie Diller

Stenhouse Publishers
Portland, Maine

To the many teachers, administrators, and children who have taught me how to make literacy work stations really work

Stenhouse Publishers
www.stenhouse.com

Copyright © 2003 by Debbie Diller

Library of Congress Cataloging-in-Publication Data
Diller, Debbie, 1954–
    Literacy work stations : making centers work / Debbie Diller.
        p. cm.
        Includes bibliographical references (p.).
        ISBN 1-57110-353-8 (alk. paper)
        1. Language arts (Elementary) 2. Education, Elementary—Activity programs. I. Title.
LB1576.D4646 2003
372.6—dc21   2003041568

Icon illustration by Carol Wetterauer

Manufactured in the United States of America on acid-free paper
09 08 07 06 05 04 9 8 7 6

Contents

Acknowledgments

This book has been the collaborative effort of many people from all over the United States. First thanks go to David Bird, Mickey Nissley, and Jane Smart, my early childhood professors from Millersville University in Pennsylvania. They laid the foundation for all I do today.

I am grateful to my dear friend and colleague Noel Gray, who made me write this book. While seated beside her at a literacy workshop, she whispered, "You must write about literacy work stations. My teachers need this piece." She encouraged me to send out the proposal that now stands before you as this book.

Special thanks to Drake Sharp, who asked me to be the "literacy work stations queen" of Alief ISD in Houston and to develop a district training program eight years ago. Also, heartfelt appreciation to Judy Wallis, for the incredible training she provided in both Alief ISD and Spring Branch ISD. She brought to life the professional books I was reading by inviting Dick Allington, Ralph Fletcher, Stephanie Harvey, Eric Jensen, Ellin Keene, Taffy Raphael, and Shane Templeton to our schools. These authors have deeply influenced my thinking and teaching.

My sincere appreciation goes to Debbie Denson, Dianne Frasier, and Peg Hill for believing in me and helping me find my focus and strengths. They deepened my understanding of the reading process and how to help struggling students.

Thanks from the bottom of my heart to all the teachers who have attended my workshops and training courses. They asked the tough questions and helped me understand how to make literacy work stations really work. A special thanks to the many teachers who allowed me to walk through their classrooms, make suggestions, move furniture, and take photos.

Over the years several masterful teachers made their classrooms available to me as "test kitchens." We spent hours during and after school trying to figure out how to teach with literacy work stations. A huge thank-you to them: Leigh Benson, Michelle Cheslock, Kathleen DiFelice, Pam House, Janet Jones, Debbie Lea, Robin McDaniel, and Dawn Vela.

My friend Patty Terry, pictured on the front cover, continues to inspire me. Thank you for always letting me try out new ideas with your students. You are the "pied piper" of first grade.

Thanks especially for all the photo shoots you let me set up in your classroom and for getting the photo permissions from every student so they could be included in this book.

I owe many thanks to the administrators who welcomed me into their districts and buildings to teach and learn about literacy work stations, especially those who let me come in time after time to pursue my study at a deeper level: Cathy Airola, Kelly Andrews, Cindy Blankenship, Brenda Emanuel, Ilene Fields, Linda Green, Holly Hughes, Julia Kerr, Jennifer Mauldin, Ed Mills, JoAnn Parrish, Janet Penner, Denise Petri, Debbie Phillips, Sandra Sandoval, Dolores Stoughton, Carol Suell, and Beverly Walker. A special thanks to Janine Hoke, my principal, who believed I could make a difference.

Hugs to my friend Olga McLaren and the Harvard Educators' Forum, a dedicated group of teacher-researchers who support my work. And deep appreciation to my friend and mentor John O'Flahavan, who always asks me if I've carved out time to write. He encourages me to think deeply about the social destination of all I ask children to do.

I am also indebted to the following friends: Lorena Barreno (and others in Spring Branch ISD) for the Spanish translations; Terri Beeler for all our walks and talks about writing; Nancy Considine of QEP Books for constantly asking me when I was going to write a book so she could sell it: she graciously set up a breakfast meeting with Stenhouse at an International Reading Association conference; Betsy Franco, who told me I was a writer and made me believe I had stories to tell; Janette Smith, who does anything I need—from mailing manuscripts to checking reference dates—with a smile; Jan Tucker, who keeps me thinking forward and guides me to work smarter, not harder; Tangye Stephney, who always checks to be sure I'm writing and who reminds me who, I'm doing this for and what kind of work it is; and Carol Wetterauer, who drew the icons under huge time constraints.

During the writing of this book I have weathered much—starting two new businesses (my husband's and mine), surviving two major computer crashes, getting a Great Dane puppy, remodeling my office and living room, and sending my oldest to college. Thanks to all who helped me through these transitions, especially Karla Pitts and my Grace Group "compadres" for their prayer support.

I feel blessed to work with the best in the industry—Philippa Stratton, who took a chance on me. Thank you for your kind and thoughtful direction as I learned to write a chapter book. Thanks to Tom Seavey for your marketing expertise and to Martha Drury for designing a cover that took my breath away and for finding a way to include the many photos that teachers ask for. Thank you to Donna Bouvier for your careful copyediting that made this book even better.

Thank you to the children. They always show me the way. When I step back and watch them, they always tell me what to do next.

And last, but not least, thanks to my family: Tom, Jon, and Jessica for your love and laughter. You mean the world to me!

What Is a
Literacy Work Station?

It's the end of summer. School begins in just a few weeks. At night as you sleep, you find yourself dreaming about your new classroom, how it will be different this year. You see yourself sitting at the guided reading table with five young students gathered around you ready to read a new book. As you introduce the new text, no one interrupts you. There is no "Teacher, I need help with this paper," "The headset at the listening station doesn't work," or "He hit me!"

You glance around the room and see the rest of the class working cheerfully and intently at reading and writing tasks that the children find purposeful and fully engaging. Two boys stand beside the overhead, which is projecting a poem onto a nearby screen. Together they read this poem, which had been introduced to the class during shared reading. Then the pair take a dry-erase marker and circle the rhyming words. They read the rhyming words together and use magnetic letters to make other words that rhyme with those from the poem. They copy their rhyming words onto strips of paper, which they put in their literacy work station folders.

You smile and return your gaze to the small group you're sitting with. You observe which children are using the strategies you've been modeling. You guide their reading and prompt when necessary, watching your students in the process of becoming independent problem solvers. At the end of your guided reading group, students move to different work stations and the learning continues.

Is this just a dream? It doesn't need to be. This is the type of classroom I have been helping teachers establish in my work as a literacy coach. My own classrooms certainly had their share of off-task behavior and constant interruptions. But over the years, collaborating with groups of teachers all across the nation, I've learned what makes independent work successful in K–2 classrooms.

When I began teaching kindergarten over twenty-five years ago, my learning centers were organized around such activities as block building, housekeeping, art, and discovery. (I also had a teacher center.) Each week I changed activities at the centers and tried to tie them to themes of study. I rotated the children from center to center daily. It was a lot of work coming up with new ideas every week! And the children didn't have much time for reading or writing practice.

A few years later, when I taught third grade, I still had learning centers—for children who finished their work. After the students did their worksheets, they could play folder games, work on a literature-related project, or read with a partner. I looked at centers as an "extra," an incentive to help kids get their work done.

How my thinking has evolved over the years! About eight years ago, the director of kindergarten for my school district approached me to develop a new approach to learning centers that would better meet the needs of all students. We decided to try literacy work stations, changing the name from *centers* to *work stations* to show that the focus would be on the child's work. I believe that independent work should be meaningful to students (as well as to the teacher). When we began to use the term with children, it seemed to remind them that what goes on is their work. Yes, many times what they do in the work stations looks like play. But when students are engaged in learning, it is more than play. It is meaningful practice that allows the learning to take root in the child's brain.

Engaging the Brain

The term *work stations* also helps remind teachers that these are not an extra. They are not something students turn to when their work is finished. Work stations are for all children. The tasks that students do at their work stations take the place of worksheets. The emphasis is on hands-on learning that engages students.

Eric Jensen writes about getting the brain's attention in his book *Teaching with the Brain in Mind* (1998). He suggests that to increase students' intrinsic motivation and keep their attention, teachers should provide choices, make learning relevant and personal, and make it engaging (emotional, ener-

getic, physical). These are exactly the factors that make literacy work stations successful in classrooms.

Jensen writes that a change in location is one of the easiest ways to get the brain's attention. At literacy work stations, students move to various places in the classroom to participate in learning with partners. He also suggests that teachers provide a rich balance of novelty and ritual. In contrast to seatwork, literacy work stations provide novelty as children partake in a variety of tasks around the classroom. In each chapter that follows I show how to maintain novelty in work stations and thus engage students (and reduce behavior problems).

Teachers can do much to set up success for students by considering what students pay attention to and what engages them. To increase students' attention to tasks, have them:

- Play a game.

- Make something.

- Talk with a partner.

- Tell a story.

- Be a recorder (have a job to do).

- Move.

- Do something new.

Literacy work stations provide all of the above and more.

Definition

A literacy work station is an area within the classroom where students work alone or interact with one another, using instructional materials to explore and expand their literacy. It is a place where a variety of activities reinforce and/or extend learning, often without the assistance of the classroom teacher. It is a time for children to practice reading, writing, speaking, listening, and working with letters and words.

Let's break down this definition and take a closer look at each part of what constitutes a literacy work station.

An Area Within the Classroom

One problem teachers usually mention is that they don't have enough space in their classrooms for literacy work stations. Yet these stations can be created by utilizing existing classroom furniture and don't take up much extra room. For example, if you have a Big Book easel, you have a Big Book work station. Your tape recorder becomes a listening station. Classroom computers make up your computer sta-

tion. An overhead projector becomes an overhead work station. Literacy work stations save classroom space. They are not an extra; they are an integral part of instruction. The following chapters include instructions on how to set up each literacy work station using existing classroom space.

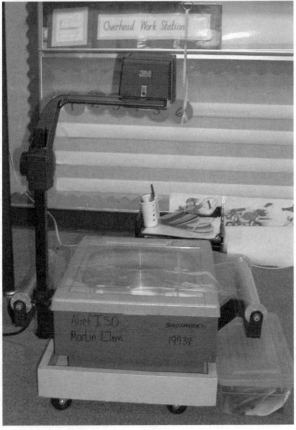

Existing classroom equipment is used for work stations: a Big Book easel becomes a Big Book work station; a tape recorder stored on the bottom of a TV cart becomes a listening work station; an overhead projector becomes the overhead work station.

Working Alone or with Partners

Many teachers tell me that their classrooms get too noisy when their children use work stations. To decrease the noise level, try reducing the number of children working together. In literacy work stations, most children work in pairs, especially at the start of the school year. Sometimes I allow students to work alone. Some children prefer working solo and are less distracted when doing so. Remember that there are other times during the day for small-group work, such as in a social studies project, a science experiment, or a game in P.E.

Using Instructional Materials

Instructional materials already used in teaching go into the work stations. The idea is for the teacher to model how to use the materials first, using them with the students to be sure they understand how to use them, then moving these materials into the work stations for independent practice. I used to make and use lots of games with file folders, but I found that the children who were most successful with them were usually the ones who didn't need the practice! Today I prefer teaching a word study game to a large or small group as part

Modeling a lesson with the word wall that is later practiced at the ABC/word study work station.

of my instructional time with them and then moving the game into the work station for independent practice.

For example, during large-group time we work with the word wall. Using Patricia Cunningham's ideas, I introduce five new words by spelling the words aloud, giving each a cheer after we clap and spell it ("L-i-g-h-t, light—yay, light!"), and playing "guess the word" where I give clues and children try to guess the word. In this way students automatically have several activities they can do at the ABC/word study work station, which is located by the word wall. Patricia Cunningham's *Phonics They Use* (1995) and Janiel Wagstaff's *Teaching Reading and Writing with Word Walls* (1999) are two excellent resources for other ways to use the word wall instructionally.

Variety of Activities

Choice is an important feature in making literacy work stations successful. A station should include a variety of things for children to choose from, but there shouldn't be so many choices that the children feel overwhelmed. Aim for what I call "controlled choice." Provide several choices of activities within a work station. Any of the activities there should accomplish the practice the child needs; but allowing the child to choose the activity will enable him or her to learn more. The following chapters present ideas for helping teacher and students work together to negotiate a list of possible choices for activities at each work station.

Time for Children to Practice

The emphasis at literacy work stations is on practice—meaningful, independent practice. It is a time for children to practice all that the teacher has been modeling. Thus, activities placed at the literacy work stations grow out of what the teacher has done during read-aloud, shared reading, modeled writing, shared writing, small-group instruction, and so on. Things aren't put into the work stations just to keep children busy.

Literacy Work Stations Versus Traditional Learning Centers

A literacy work station is fundamentally different from a traditional learning center in several ways, as shown in Figure 1.1. The emphasis in literacy work stations is on teacher modeling and students taking responsibility for their own learning. In traditional learning centers, teachers often did too much of the work. They would, for example, think of ideas for the materials, make the materials, laminate them, cut them out, explain them, explain them again, and clean up after the materials were used. In addition, teachers would decide when to change the materials (usually every Friday afternoon) and what would be done with them. In literacy work stations, students share in the decision making. They help decide when to change materials, and they negoti-

ate ideas for what they'd like to practice at each station. No longer does the teacher change the centers weekly. This process is explained in more detail in Chapter 2.

There are many other benefits to teaching with literacy work stations. My favorite is that *all* students get to participate in work stations for equal amounts of time. The natural result of this is that the children will usually work harder because they are doing something they enjoy. No longer will you have bored students squirming in their seats or children popping up and down asking you endless questions about how to do this paper. Nor will you have children who speed through their work carelessly so they can go to centers. All students have equal access to the engagement that literacy work stations provide.

Another benefit is that literacy work stations allow you to differentiate for the various levels within a classroom. Instead of assigning the same tasks to all children, you can suggest different activities or materials for particular children so as to bet-

Figure 1.1 Differences Between Literacy Work Stations and Traditional Learning Centers

Literacy Work Stations	Traditional Learning Centers
Materials are taught with and used for instruction first. Then they are placed in the work station for independent use.	New materials were often placed in the center without first being used in teaching. The teacher may have shown how to use the materials once, but they were often introduced with all the other new center materials at one time.
Stations remain set up all year long. Materials are changed to reflect children's reading levels, strategies being taught, and topics being studied.	Centers were often changed weekly with units of study.
Stations are used for students' meaningful independent work and are an integral part of each child's instruction. All students go to work stations daily.	Centers were often used by students when they "finished their work." Centers were used for fun and motivation, for something extra.
Materials are differentiated for students with different needs and reading levels.	All students did the same activities at centers. There was not usually much differentiation.
The teacher meets with guided reading groups during literacy work stations.	If the teacher met with small groups, each group often did the same task.

ter meet their needs at a particular station. For example, at the buddy reading work station, colored dots denoting various reading levels may be placed on the books so that children can find books that are just right for them. The teacher simply needs to remind the students of what color dot they should look for. In the following chapters you will find ideas for differentiation for each specific literacy work station.

Improved student behavior is an additional plus that comes from literacy work stations. When students are involved with hands-on activities, such as making words with magnetic letters rather than filling out spelling worksheets, they generally behave better and interrupt the teacher less. Discipline problems arise during independent time when students are asked to do things that they don't find interesting or useful to their learning. Skills students would traditionally practice with paper and pencil can be made more manipulative at the work stations. For example, instead of having students fill out page after page of handwriting practice, they might accomplish the same goal by tracing letters on a handwriting transparency at the overhead work station or by copying favorite poems into a poetry notebook at the poetry work station.

Finally, students at literacy work stations internalize what is taught because they have a direct opportunity to practice a task just as the teacher modeled it. Children apply what they are learning by successfully completing tasks, such as reading and rereading a familiar Big Book at the Big Book work station or writing a book review in response to a book they read at the classroom library (just like the book review that was modeled for them the previous week following a class read-aloud). Students get to connect old learning to new. They think back to what the teacher said during modeling—for example, "Be sure to make each word match as you point. If it doesn't match up, try it again" as they point to each word in a familiar poem they are reading from a chart in the poetry work station. Best of

all, students in work stations are constantly reading and writing. I have never seen as much reading and writing practice anywhere during independent time as I've seen during literacy work stations in the classrooms where I've coached.

Guaranteeing Independence

One huge benefit of using literacy work stations in your classroom is that children will learn to work more independently. However, to help students learn how to take on more independence, several conditions must be in place. Teachers must model appropriate behavior, allow for a gradual release of responsibility, provide a risk-free environment and a proper independent work level, and communicate clear, explicit expectations.

Modeling

Teacher modeling helps ensure independent learning. Students need to see many demonstrations of how to use materials or do tasks before they can do them well on their own. Simply showing something once isn't enough for most learners, even adult learners. Brian Cambourne's Conditions of Learning model (1988) identifies demonstration as an important prerequisite for language learning. I have found that the most successful work stations are those using materials and activities that teachers have modeled the most.

Gradual Release of Responsibility

The best way to guarantee success at literacy work stations is through lots of modeling, with teachers gradually releasing more responsibility to the children. Pearson and Gallagher's Gradual Release Model of Instruction (1983) outlines this principle (see Figure 1.2). My favorite example of how I used the gradual release model to teach a new behavior is when I taught my teenage daughter how to do

Figure 1.2 Gradual Release of Responsibility Approach

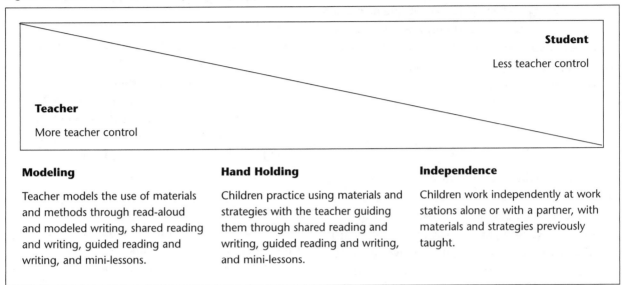

Student

Less teacher control

Teacher

More teacher control

Modeling	**Hand Holding**	**Independence**
Teacher models the use of materials and methods through read-aloud and modeled writing, shared reading and writing, guided reading and writing, and mini-lessons.	Children practice using materials and strategies with the teacher guiding them through shared reading and writing, guided reading and writing, and mini-lessons.	Children work independently at work stations alone or with a partner, with materials and strategies previously taught.

the laundry. First, she needed to learn about the materials to be used and to know what it looked like to do the laundry. She'd had fourteen years of "modeled laundry," so it was on to the next step! Next, we did "shared laundry." While we sorted the clothes together, I explained how to separate dark colors from white and told her why this was important. I set the temperatures while she watched, and again I explained why I used each temperature. (Since she bought some of her own clothes, she had a vested interest in the "whys.") In a few weeks we moved on to "guided laundry." Now she sorted and I checked; she set the temperature on the washer and dryer, and I checked; she hung the all-cotton pieces on hangers to dry, and I checked. When I was satisfied with her performance, she finally moved to "independent laundry." I was sure she could do it on her own, because I had *gradually* released the responsibility to her.

To best train students for literacy work stations, teachers do the same thing. They begin by modeling—showing students how to do something, such as how to read a transparency of a new poem on the overhead projector: that is, placing the transparency on the overhead, turning on the machine,

reading the poem to the class and inviting the students to join in if they'd like, then returning the poem to a folder labeled "Overhead Poems" after projecting and reading it. Then, as the teacher shares the reading of the poem with the children the following day, he or she gradually turns over more responsibility to them to do the reading. The support of all the students reading together builds their confidence and skill. The teacher may ask one of them to turn on the overhead or to put the poem back in its folder. Eventually, students can read the poem fluently and with good expression on their own because of the way the teacher scaffolded the event for them. They know how to use the equipment because the teacher has shared the responsibility with them. At this point, the poem can be moved into the overhead work station for independent practice.

Risk-Free Environment

Another of Cambourne's Conditions of Learning (1988) is referred to as *approximations*. Students are encouraged to "have a go" at tasks as they practice them. Students learn best in a classroom where they feel safe and secure. They often learn more when working with a peer to practice something new. Eric Jensen (1998) notes that the brain learns best when threats are removed. Grading what children practice is threatening. Use grades judiciously at work stations. Carefully select products to grade after students have had opportunities to practice.

Independent Work Level

Sometimes children get into trouble at a work station when they cannot do a task independently because it's too difficult for them. Once at the beginning of second grade, I decided to put what I thought were "easy" poems into the overhead station for practice, even though we'd never read them together during shared reading time. What a big mistake! A few of the children couldn't read the poems and got frustrated while working there. Subsequently, they began misbehaving. This should have been no surprise. Yet, I see this mistake happen often in classrooms I work in. When the task is too hard, when the children don't thoroughly understand the task, or when the purpose of the task is unclear, the result is often off-task behavior and teacher interruptions.

Russian psychologist Lev Vygotsky (1978) explained that student learning takes place in the child's "zone of proximal development," or ZPD. Activities in the ZPD are just a little bit beyond the child's developmental level (that is, a bit beyond what the child can do totally independently), things the child can do with the support of a peer. Sometimes the ZPD is explained as what children can do with support today that they can do on their own tomorrow. Social interaction is utilized to further the learning within the child's ZPD. Just a bit beyond a child's ZPD lies frustration. If you closely examine students who get into trouble in class, chances are you'll find that some of them are being asked to function at a level above their current ZPD. This is why differentiation at literacy work stations is so critical.

Clear, Explicit Expectations

When I observe in classrooms, I sometimes notice stations that aren't working well at all. I ask the children what they're supposed to be doing at that work station. Many times they don't know. For example, in one second-grade room the word study station was very noisy. I asked the students to tell me about what they were doing there. They said, "I don't know." I showed them how to play one of the games and joined them for a few minutes in the game. Then I let them work on their own. They were fine after that.

In this book you will find suggestions for an "I Can" list to post at each work station. The list outlines what students can do at the station, which helps clarify expectations. Because the lists are developed with the students, they will better understand what to do at each work station.

An "I Can" list made with students posted at the classroom library.

Non-Negotiables for Literacy Work Stations

Not long after September 11 I heard Shelley Harwayne, superintendent of the New York City schools, speak about writing. She said that the tragedy had made her more closely examine what she believed about many things, and she then presented her non-negotiables for writing. Her talk made me think deeply about what I believed were the most important components of literacy work stations, and as soon as I got back to my hotel room I created a list of my own—my non-negotiables for literacy work stations.

Focus on practice and purposes, not the "stuff" of stations. One evening a dear friend called and asked if I could make a list for every six weeks of what needed to be placed in each work station in first grade. Her request made me think about what we often focus on in our lesson planning. Too many times we begin with the "stuff." Many times when I give workshops, teachers ask me to just give them activities.

My thinking is just the opposite. I believe that if you begin with what it is you're trying to teach—your purpose—then you can more easily figure out which materials to use. This book is organized to help you think about what your students need and to plan for the "stuff" accordingly.

Link to your teaching. When student practice is directly tied to instruction, you get more bang for your teaching buck. For example, you read aloud a picture book. Then you do shared writing of a personal response to that book. During this time you model how to write about favorite parts of a book, including examples students give you. If you have a special form for students to use for this piece of writing, you show them an enlarged model of that form. After you've shared the writing of several responses over several days, you move the personal

Class follow-up writing to a read-aloud of *Wemberley Worries* posted at the classroom library.

response sheets into the classroom library or listening work station.

Slow down to speed up. When I ask teachers at the end of the year what they might do differently next year, they invariably tell me they will start out more slowly. They have come to recognize the value of starting out at a reduced pace and building momentum after establishing a strong foundation. They will not put out too many materials at once and will make sure that they have taught with what they place in the work stations.

In their book *Guided Reading* (1996), Irene Fountas and Gay Su Pinnell recommend spending the first six weeks of first grade establishing routines for independent learning before pulling small guided reading groups. In kindergarten it takes even longer!

Balance process and product. Some teachers try to have students create a product at every center. I think this is counterproductive and makes too much work for the teacher. Celebrate the process of learning to read and write by letting students engage in practicing reading and writing! For example, at the Big Book work station, much of the time students will read Big Books together. As they read they are improving fluency and using phonics skills. This is much more effective practice for developing proficient readers than filling out pages in workbooks.

Include a balance of process and product. Include opportunities to create products at some, but not all, stations. Use the forms in the appendixes to assess your students' progress in reading and writing. Use conventional methods to grade some student products.

Less is more. Don't put out too much stuff at once. Sometimes teachers get upset because students aren't doing a good job of keeping centers tidy when there are just too many materials for the children to manage easily. If you notice this problem, scale back on the amount of materials you have provided at the station. The same rule of thumb applies to the classroom library. Don't put out your entire collection of 200 books at the start of the year and expect kindergartners to keep them orderly. Start small and add things over time.

Use novelty. Novelty gets students' attention (Jensen 1998), but this feature is often underutilized in our classrooms. Then again, we teachers love to get new ideas at workshops, and sometimes we return to our classrooms and try everything at once. When we do that, we actually exhaust the novelty. Try one new thing at a time. Introduce one new task or material at a time, and the novelty will last longer.

Simplify. Over the years I have tried many schemes for classroom management and have found that the simplest methods are usually the best. Keep your management system simple. Keep your materials simple, too. My cardinal rule is that if it takes longer to make something than it does for children to use it instructionally, then don't bother making it.

Making It Personal

As you read this book, make it personal. Feel free to write notes in the margins. Ask questions that pop into your mind as you read and discuss them with a colleague. If what you're already doing in your classroom is working effectively for your students, don't change it just because of this book. Use the parts that work for you and your students. Remember, there is no one way that will help each child. Follow the lead of your students. Ask for their input. They will show you the way.

Reflection and Dialogue

To help you make the most of the ideas presented in this book, each chapter concludes with a list of ideas for discussion and questions for personal reflection. Here is the list for this chapter.

1. Share your new ideas about literacy work stations with a colleague. Discuss the definition of work stations provided in this chapter (on page 2).
2. Think about your students and their level of engagement. What specific things most engaged them recently? Make a list of these and continue to plan similar kinds of activities.
3. Try using the gradual release of responsibility approach. Think about something new you've learned to do and how you probably went through a similar process. Plan for your first work stations using this model.
4. Make a list of your non-negotiables for your classroom. Determining these early in the year will help you create a successful plan. Share your list with someone from your grade level and discuss your ideas. Post your list somewhere in your classroom where you can see it as a daily reminder.

How Do I Use
Literacy Work Stations?

The question teachers most frequently ask about literacy work stations is "How do I manage them?" But I think the best answer to that is another question: "How do I teach with them?" Instruction that is explicit and well planned is a prerequisite to effective management of literacy work stations. Teachers should think through exactly what they want students to learn at a work station and how to accomplish those goals.

I often suggest that teachers brainstorm with children what a particular literacy work station should look like, sound like, and feel like. This helps both the teacher and the students understand the expectations at the station, which increases the likelihood that it will run more efficiently and effectively. Work with your students to create a list using language they understand. Here are some typical things your students might say as they help you make this chart:

In Our Classroom, Literacy Work Stations Should

Look Like:
Kids are reading.
Kids are writing.
Kids are listening.
Kids are talking with their
    partners.
Things are put back in their place.
Kids stay at their assigned station.
Kids are on task.
Teacher is not interrupted while
    working with a group.

Sound Like:
Quiet voices so others can learn.
Lots of reading.
Talking about books ("I like the
    part . . .").
Talking with just your partner.
Making choices together ("Let's
    try this.").

Feel Like:
I can do it!
I like to read and write.
Calm.
Comfortable.

Using Mini-Lessons

Beginning literacy work station time with a brief mini-lesson, or model, will provide focus and direction to the day's independent practice and help the task become more meaningful. During a mini-lesson you can show children exactly what you expect them to do at a literacy work station. Whenever you introduce a new task or tool, take a few minutes to show and tell kids how they can use it at the work station. The key to successful mini-lessons is that they be *short* and *focused,* no more than five to ten minutes in length. (Most students' attention span is not much longer than that.)

There are three different times to use a mini-lesson: when you're first introducing the work station; when you're adding something new to a station; and when you're reviewing a work station activity. Teachers often assume that they can introduce an activity just once and have students do it successfully. This is a mistake; I have found that children need many models on an ongoing basis.

Mini-Lessons at the Beginning of the School Year

At the start of the year, the mini-lessons you will need to conduct are different from those you'll do later in the year. You might teach one of the mini-lessons suggested below daily for the first two weeks of school. (For more ideas, refer to the "How to Introduce the Work Station" and "What the Teacher Needs to Model" sections in Chapters 3 to 8.) *Do not assume that students who have used work stations in first grade will know exactly what you expect them to do with them in second grade!*

Begin by having students sit close to you on the floor. Tell them explicitly what you expect them to do. Then have two children role-play while the rest of the group observes. Have the observers tell what they noticed. For example, after you have modeled and explained to children how to use the tape

Whole-class mini-lesson on how to use the listening work station.

recorder at the listening work station, have two students show the rest of the class what it would look like if they were now at that station. It might sound something like this:

Child 1: Let's listen to *The Three Bears* tape. I like that story.
Child 2: Okay. I'll put the tape in.
Child 1: Here's your book. I'll push the green button to make it start.
Child 2: Remember to turn the page with the beep.

The children listen to a bit of the tape and turn the pages when the recording signals them to do so. After a minute or so, stop them and ask them to pretend they are finished. Their dialogue continues:

Child 1: I started the tape, so you can push the red button to make it stop.
Child 2: I have to rewind it, too, so the tape will be ready for the next kids who come here.
Child 1: Push the yellow button to rewind. I'll put the tape and books back in the tub.
Child 2: That was a good story. I hope we get to listen to it again.

Two children role-play how to use the listening work station.

The two children doing the demonstration now remain standing while the others give them feedback. Give several children a chance to tell what they noticed that the role-modeling students did. Comments might include: "I liked the way they took turns with the buttons"; "They did a good job of cleaning up"; "They remembered to rewind the tape when they were done"; "They were good listeners." Thank the students for their participation and remind the class to do exactly what they saw modeled today when they work at this station.

Here's what you might say in each role-play scenario:

■ *How to use the equipment/materials.* "You may use markers at the writing station. You can write with them gently and the ink will come out easily. You don't need to push hard on them. That will ruin them. When you're finished, put the lid on tightly. Listen for the 'click' to know that you've put it on right.

Mario and Suzanne, please show us how you might use the markers at the writing work station."

■ *How to share materials.* "There are plenty of materials, but you will have to share. If somebody wants something that you want, too, use a problem-solving strategy. Don't take too much of something, or there won't be enough for anyone else. Bill and Deondra, pretend that you are at the ABC/word study station stamping out spelling words, and you both want the same stamp at the same time."

■ *How to take turns.* "You will be working with a partner, so you will have to take turns. Decide who will go first and then let the other one go. Switch back and forth. If one of you goes first today, let the other one go first tomorrow. To decide who goes first, you might play Paper, Rock, Scissors or flip a coin. Or you could both write your name on a piece of paper from the scrap box, then pull one name to decide who goes first. If you're having trouble with someone taking too long, use an egg timer. Let each person's turn last as long as the egg timer. Then let the other one have a turn. Renee and Sophie, show us what it would look like if you were having trouble taking turns and solved your problem."

■ *How to use the management board.* "We will be using a board to help us know which work stations we should work at today. First find your name to see whom you will work with. Then look at the icons to see which stations you will go to. Go to the first station and work there until you hear my bell ring. Then switch and go to the next station pictured by your name on the management board. Leticia and Juan, please go to the management board and show us how to do this. Find your names, then go to your first station. Listen for the bell, and then switch to your next work station." (Icons are used to help identify work stations. See Appendix A for sample icons. Management boards are explained later in this chapter.)

■ *How to use the "I Can" list.* (See Chapters 3–8 for specific ideas for "I Can" lists for each station.) "As a class, we wrote a list of things you might do at the classroom library. Some days you might not know what you want to do there. So you can just look at the list to help you choose something to do. Let's read the 'I Can' list for the classroom library. Now, Stevie and Jennifer, go to the classroom library and pretend that you don't know what to do today. Show us what you can do to help yourself."

■ *How to solve a problem.* "Sometimes a problem may come up at your work station. Maybe a tape breaks at the listening station or you run out of paper at the writing station or someone

says mean words to you at buddy reading. What do you do? There are many ways to solve a problem. If something breaks or you run out of something, ask a materials manager for help. If someone is mean to you, tell that person that his or her words are hurting you and to please stop. If that child doesn't stop, take your work to your desk and finish it there until it is time to switch stations. If your problem has to do with taking turns, remember the ways we have to solve that problem." In addition to having children role-play solving problems that may come up, you might also write a chart together that explains what to do in a given situation (see Figure 2.1).

■ *Where can I go for help?* "If you need help with materials or something breaks, ask a materials manager. If you have trouble with the computer, ask the computer expert. If you don't know how to figure out a word in reading and

Figure 2.1 How to Solve Problems

What Is Happening	How to Solve the Problem
You run out of something, like paper.	Ask a materials manager for help.
Something breaks or doesn't work right.	Ask a materials manager for help.
Someone says something mean to you.	Tell the person to stop, that his or her words are hurting you. If he or she doesn't stop, take your work to your desk and work alone.
You can't decide who should go first.	Play Paper, Rock, Scissors.
	Let the person whose name starts with the first letter of the alphabet go first.
	Each of you write your name on a piece of paper and fold it. Pick one name and read it. That person goes first this time.
Someone hits you.	Tell the person to stop. Then go to your desk to work until it's time to switch to your next work station.
You don't know what to do at the work station.	Read the "I Can" list for an idea.
	Ask your partner what to do.

A materials manager and a computer helper minimize teacher interruptions during work station time.

writing, ask your partner. Please do not ask me for help while I'm working with a small group. You don't like it when someone interrupts your group. Patrice and Luis, please pretend like you're having a problem at the overhead station. Then show us how to get help without interrupting the teacher." Debbie Miller, in *Reading with Meaning* (2002), noted a great solution that her students came up with for the "how do I get help" problem. If there's something that only the teacher can help you with, they suggested, write her a little note and stick it on the dry-erase board so that when she is free, she can read it. They added, "Be sure to sign your name."

■ *How to put things away.* "It's important to put things away neatly and carefully, so the next people can find and use them. Everything has a special place where it should be put away when you're done. Use the labels on the containers to help you. If you can't read the words, the pictures will help you. Remember to put things back the way you found them. The materials managers will check on literacy work stations when we're finished to be sure

we've all done a good job of getting ready for tomorrow. Blanca and Jon, please show us how to put things away at the puzzles and games station."

■ *How to switch to the next work station.* "I will ring a bell to let you know it is time to clean up. When you hear the bell, please stop and begin to clean up. Be sure to make things neat enough for the next group to use them. When I ring the bell the second time, quietly walk to your next work station. Use the management board to check where to go, if you need to. When you get to your next place, get to work right away. Sammy and Tom, show us how to switch stations. Look at the management board and show us what this would look like." An alternative to ringing a bell is to teach a predetermined signal, such as your snapping a pattern while the children repeat it. Some teachers sing a little song to let the children know it's time to move to the next station, and others ask everyone to stand up wherever they are in the room. The important thing is to teach a signal and use it consistently.

Mini-Lessons Later in the Year

You will probably be repeating many of the mini-lessons from the start of the school year throughout the year for reinforcement. If you notice that students are having trouble sharing, for example, make a note to yourself to do a mini-lesson on that the following day. Remember, much modeling produces better behavior at work stations.

In addition, there will be other kinds of mini-lessons you will be doing later in the year. These will consist of quick reviews of how to use particular materials you've already used instructionally. You'll simply remind students of how to use them on their own in the literacy work stations.

For example, you may have been reading *The Three Little Pigs* during read-aloud and have compared several versions. You have done retellings with finger puppets. You have read a reader's theater of this story in shared reading. Today you've decided to move these materials into the drama work station. Tell children that these materials will be appearing in this work station today. Remind them of how to use and care for the materials and how to put them away carefully. It is a good idea to have two children model for the class how to use these familiar materials now newly entered in the drama work station. Make sure you let the class know exactly what you expect as they practice with the new additions. Assume nothing!

Each time you place new materials in a work station, tell the students you have done so. This prepares them for the new task—and heads off any questions they may have that they'd be tempted to interrupt you with while you're working with a small group. You can mention during shared reading, for example, that you're placing last week's Big Book there. Or you might choose to re-model the task right before literacy work station time to be sure that the children know what to do. The more complex the job, the greater need there is for explicit modeling.

Management Boards

There are many types of management boards that can be used for literacy work stations. I've found that classrooms are generally more successful when a teacher uses a management board, although some highly skilled teachers can manage without them. The key is that students know where they're supposed to be, when they're supposed to be there, and what they're supposed to be doing.

The simplest type of management board is a basic pocket chart. Simply write or type each child's name on a card in large black letters and place two names in each row of the pocket chart. Beside each pair of names, place one or two icons to show where those children are to go during literacy work

Three types of management boards: posted on a magnetic chalkboard; put on a bulletin board; set up to match guided reading groups.

station time. The icons in Appendix A can be reduced to fit in a pocket chart. At the end of each day, move each pair of names down to the next space so that the children's activities change for the next day. This way you don't have to keep extra charts to be sure every child gets to go to every station. This method insures that they do. You also don't have to worry about getting all the work stations "done" in one week. You simply rotate kids from station to station; over time, they automatically get to do everything.

Begin by having each child go to one work station daily. Eventually, you may allow students to go to two or three a day. To show this, make multiple copies of each icon. Place two or three icons beside the pair of students' names to show where they will go first, second, and third. Children can read the board and know where to move when you signal for them to go to the next station. Again, simply move down the icons to the next row beside the next pair of names daily.

There are, of course, many other ways to set up management boards. The key is to find one that works for you and your students. You could, for example, use a rotation wheel. Make a large and a small laminated circle. List the stations on the outer wheel and the students' names on the inner wheel. To make the wheel easier to use, you could attach icons with Velcro to the outer wheel so they can be moved and changed. Write students' names on the inner wheel with an erasable marker so they can also be changed as partners change. Simply turn the wheel daily.

Another type of management board may be made with strips of poster board. You could make a different-colored strip to match each guided reading group. List the children's names in that group at the top of each strip and attach the icons for that day below each list, using Velcro or paper clips inserted into slits made with a cutting tool. You can change the icons daily.

Work Station Time

Each day, following the brief mini-lesson, let students review the management board and move right into their work stations. Children should know what to do and get busy right away because of the modeling you have done. At the beginning of the year, while students are learning to use the work stations, you should be circulating, observing, and giving assistance as needed. As Irene Fountas and Gay Su Pinnell recommend in their book *Guided Reading* (1996), you should not meet with small groups for guided reading until about six weeks into the school year in first and second grade (and even later in kindergarten). Only when classroom management is under control will you be able to focus on good small-group teaching. Invest the first six weeks of school in teaching routines to your students and watching them practice at literacy work stations so that you will be able to work with small groups in the following months. Once you have begun small-group instruction, you must remain aware of what students are doing at work stations. Suggestions for how to accomplish this are given in the following chapters in the section "How to Assess/Keep Kids Accountable" at each station.

Frequently Asked Questions

As you read the following, keep in mind that there is no one right answer to any of these questions. Management styles are as varied as the teachers in classrooms. There is no one ideal way of managing literacy work stations that will solve all problems. The best advice I can give is to use your common sense in dealing with challenges that arise.

How many students should work together at a station?

Most problems that occur in work stations are interpersonal. The troubles are usually among the children working there: kids don't share; they argue; they get too loud; they push or use hurtful words. Many teachers I've worked with have found that by having only two children work together at a work

Two students read familiar Big Books together at the Big Book work station.

station, noise and behavior problems are dramatically reduced. The old saying "Two's company, three's a crowd" seems to hold true in the classroom. When children work together in pairs there are often fewer problems. Of course, if you have three or four children working well together, don't change it!

In some cases, certain children work better alone at work stations. They may march to the beat of a different drummer, or they may simply prefer to work by themselves. Ryan was one of those kids. He did better when he worked on his own. When he was with a partner, he'd sometimes be gruff or impatient. When he was alone, he could focus better. He would occasionally listen to what others beside him were doing and join in, but for the most part he worked best unaccompanied. Work station time, after all, is time for independent practice, and if a child works better alone, that's fine. There will be other opportunities during the day for students to work in small groups, perhaps during science or social studies, on projects. Literacy work stations should not be the only chance during the day for kids to work in small groups.

How many work stations should I have? How often should I change them?

You must decide how many stations you and your students can handle. Many teachers have ten or more work stations set up that they use all year long. They do not change activities every Friday, so having this many students is not much work for them. The practice activities that are moved into the work stations are things that students have already learned to do with the teacher during instruction. Students practice them over and over during work station time. A variety of work stations keeps kids' interest high. You don't have to be tied into a Monday–Friday rotation, so don't worry if every child doesn't get to every work station in a week. (See Chapter 10 for more ideas on changing activities.)

How long should work station time last?

As part of a teacher research project, some first-grade teachers timed their students at literacy work stations to see when children began to get restless or problems began to erupt. They found problems starting at around thirteen minutes! Many teachers I work with change stations after fifteen or twenty minutes, which seems to be just about right.

If you let kids stay too long in one work station, behavior problems will begin to occur. It's a good idea to keep an eye on the time and move students to a new activity before trouble starts. Many teachers keep a timer by their guided reading table and set it for twenty minutes. When the bell rings, the students automatically clean up and begin moving to the next station.

Most teachers let students work at two or three work stations a day for a total of about forty-five minutes to an hour. Of course, at the beginning of the school year, literacy work station time might last just fifteen or twenty minutes, with students going to just one station.

How do I decide who should work with whom?

There are many ways to pair students. Decide on your purposes for the grouping before making decisions on who will work together. For example, if you want students to practice activities on the cutting edge of their development, if you want them to do things that are just a little challenging but are within their range of successfully accomplishing, then you might pair students reading at a similar level who need practice with the same type of thing. If two children are emergent readers and you'd like them to practice reading emergent books together, it would make sense to pair them at the buddy reading work station.

Many teachers pair students heterogeneously so they can help each other. This has its place, too. If you want children to be able to help each other by reading directions, for example, you might pair students this way.

At times, you might want students to choose their own partners. This may motivate some children because of the added choice provided.

Think carefully about how you set up your partners at work stations, and don't stick to only one way of choosing partners. Vary the pairings occasionally to keep interest high.

Should the children decide or should I choose which stations they will go to?

Research has shown that choice helps motivate students. However, when it comes to classroom management, many teachers do better initially giving children "controlled choices" at literacy work stations. It is generally easier to start the year by assigning students where you'd like them to go and eventually turning over more of the choice to them than to begin by letting everyone go wherever they'd like and ending up with chaos!

Provide choice within each literacy work station by having several open-ended activities children can choose from. This allows students to have some choice in a controlled way, which will help establish a predictable routine. For example, when a child goes to the ABC/word study station, he or she may choose to put words in alphabetical order, write words on a dry-erase board, read an alphabet book, and/or create sentences with word wall words. At the listening station, there may be three different tapes and several types of response sheets for children to choose from. In one classroom I visited, the teacher had assigned only one activity for students to do at each station. She wondered why they were getting done so fast and why she was having discipline problems. When she added more choice within the stations, her problems disappeared.

Again, it is up to you to decide how to determine which stations children go to. Teachers must know their students and what they can handle.

What if some students finish before everyone else? What if someone isn't finished when it's time to switch to another work station?

If the activities in the station are varied, open-ended, and interesting to the students, they generally won't be finished early. However, some students may become engaged in an activity and not be ready to move on to the next station. Be flexible! Allow the child to take his or her work to a desk to finish, and skip that next rotation for that student. (One exception to this is the computer station, because of the limited time available.)

What if students misbehave during literacy work station time?

Children sometimes don't do what they're expected to during work station time. They should be made aware beforehand of what they are supposed to do and what will happen if they break the rules. I use the "one strike and you're out" rule in literacy stations. This time is highly motivating to the children, and they don't like to miss it. So if they know the teacher means business, they will be more likely to do what is expected. I simply tell students, "This is what you may do at the stations. This is what you may *not* do. If you break the rules, you will have to leave the station at once." I don't give idle threats or warnings. I tell them what I expect and then I follow through.

Most teachers have found that simply having a chair or two by their guided reading table for children who have not followed the rules works best. When I sent students back to their desks to put their heads down, they still acted out and wanted my attention. But if I sat them near me but didn't involve them in my lesson, they tended to pay attention to what the other students were doing and may have even learned something from this vicarious learning experience!

One teacher shared with me a surefire method for discipline in her class during literacy work station time. If kids had to be removed from stations due to poor behavior, she had them take a piece of paper and draw a picture of how their behavior would change when they returned to that station. Notice that she didn't ask them to write, nor was she "punishing" them. She was simply asking them to reflect on their behavior in a nonthreatening

way. She said that many times students began writing spontaneously about their behavior after they drew. In fact, she got some of her best writing samples from some of her "behaviorally challenged" students this way.

If you find the same students having to be removed from work stations day after day, take a look at those individuals. You may want to design an individualized plan to help them get back on track. (See Chapter 10 for suggestions on setting up individualized plans.)

Folders and Finished Work Boxes

At some literacy work stations students might create products. For example, at the writing station, students may make a card or write a story. At the ABC/word study station, they might write spelling words with markers. When children create products at a given work station, they will need a special place to store these products. There are three main ways to handle storage:

1. If you want a central storage place to hold everybody's work, keep a box or tray labeled "Finished Work" into which students place completed products. You may then simply pick up the work at the end of the day to check it.
2. You can collect the products at each station. You can have a Finished Work tray or box at each work station that might have a product. This way the products are presorted by work station.
3. If you want individual storage, a double pocket folder with brads for each child works well. Students can place completed work or work in progress in the pockets of the folder. If you use a management sheet to keep track of what each student has done, you can three-hole-punch the sheet and place it in the folder, secured by the brads. Use the sheets in Appendix A for the Finished Work folders.

Storing finished work: centrally located basket; basket at the ABC/word study work station; folder for storing individual student's finished work.

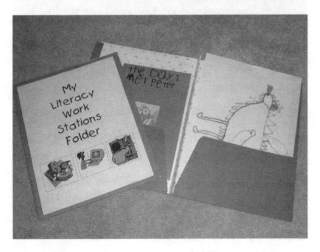

It is not necessary to use individual management sheets. Some teachers prefer to use them, while others keep track by watching their management board. If you are simply rotating kids from one station to the next, there is no need to have an extra sheet for each student.

Sharing Time

Following work station time, it is useful to have a brief sharing time with the class. This provides an opportunity for students to reflect on what they've done that day and help their learning go deeper. During sharing time, gather the students on the floor in a central meeting place, much as you did during the mini-lesson. This time, lead a *short, focused* discussion about what they did and learned in the work stations. You might find it useful to have one specific question to reflect on each day. Here are some possibilities:

■ What did I do at the work stations today?

■ What did I have fun doing at the work stations today?

■ What didn't I like at the work stations today?

■ What did I do to help myself become a better reader today?

■ What did I do to help myself become a better writer today?

■ What do I think we should change at the work stations?

■ What else would I like to do at the work stations?

■ How did I solve a problem at the work stations today?

■ How did I help someone else solve a problem at the work stations today?

These and other questions may be copied onto cards, secured with a ring, and used to lead the sharing time discussion.

In kindergarten at the beginning of the school year, you will have to model how to answer these questions. For example, you might say, "We're going to talk about what you did at the literacy work stations today. This will give you some ideas of what you might try when you work at them tomorrow. I saw Jasmine writing the names of her friends at the writing work station. She used the name cards to help her. She used one of the new fancy pencils I put in the station to write with. I watched Marcus at the classroom library. He read the new Clifford book that I read to you during read-aloud last week. He doesn't know how to read all the words yet, so he turned the pages carefully and told the story of Clifford as he looked at the pictures. Who can tell me something they did at the work stations today? I'll call on three children today, and tomorrow we'll do it again and more of you will have a turn to tell what you did."

Early in the year in first and second grade, sharing time may resemble the following scenario:

Teacher: What did you like doing at the work stations today?

Sharing time after literacy work station time.

Amber: I really liked reading with Mrs. Diller in our reading group. We read a whole bunch and nobody interrupted us. I got to learn to read better today.

Teacher: Thank you for doing such a good job of working independently at the work stations today. The students in the group did learn a lot today. Keep up the good work of solving problems on your own. That way everyone can learn.

Jess: I liked reading *Silly Sally* at the Big Book station. I read with David, and we used voices that sounded like the characters. We used the puppets to act out the story while we read, too.

Teacher: *Silly Sally* is a funny book, isn't it? Reading with expression and using the characters' voices makes the reading more interesting. The puppets help to tell the story. I hope more of you will read this book this week and remember to use those characters' voices!

Max: My favorite thing today was the drama station. Will and I did a play about rain. It was the play we did in class during shared reading. We really liked being the different parts. There were three parts, so I did two and Will did one. Then we read it again, and I did one part and Will did two. It was fun to take turns.

Teacher: You made good choices today. It's fun to read plays at the drama station. I like the way you took turns. I know that made it more fun, too. After lunch, would you like to do the play for the class?

Solving Ongoing Problems

Problems students mention during sharing time can become the next day's mini-lessons. For example, when Roberto said he didn't like that someone played the tape at the listening station too loudly, I taught how to use the tape recorder the next day as the mini-lesson. When two students said that they got in trouble because they were tired of the same old poems at the poetry work station, the next day I added some new ones we'd just read in shared reading. In the mini-lesson I introduced the new poems.

Although good teaching should head off many problems, trouble will still brew from time to time. When a problem arises at work stations, begin by looking at what might have caused it. The first place to look is at your own teaching. (Ouch!) I used to look at the students first until I realized that most problems were related to my instruction.

Ask yourself:

■ How did I model this new task or use of materials?

■ Did I model enough? Should I re-model?

■ How long has this material been in the work station? (It might be time to replace it to keep interest high.)

■ Are the materials at the work station well organized and easy to use?

■ Have I recently had the children change partners? Is it time for new partners? Would someone work better alone?

■ Is there an "I Can" list in the station? Does it need to be updated?

■ Is there enough for students to do at this station? What materials need to be changed or added?

■ Can the children do this activity on their own?

■ Is the activity interesting and meaningful to the child? If not, what can I change to make it so?

In one first-grade classroom I visited, I noticed that the pocket chart station was closed down. (For more on this type of work station, see Chapter 9.) When I asked the teacher why, she replied, "They just don't know how to use it, so I shut it down!" Out of frustration, we are often tempted to simply close down centers. I asked her what the students had been doing there. She said that she had some poems on sentence strips for kids to put in order and read, but that they just got in trouble when they were there. There was little or no reading going on; she saw the children at that work station poking each other with the wooden pointers. A definite problem, I agreed.

I brainstormed with this teacher how she could reopen the center. First we looked at the task. The kids were bored with it. The poems had been there for a while and there was no challenge or motivation associated with this station any longer. I suggested that she change the task. She had been using Patricia Cunningham's *Making Words* (1994) in class. They really enjoyed this gamelike activity. "Why don't you move that task into the pocket chart station for practice?" I suggested. She loved the idea. I reminded her that anything that can be sorted, sequenced, or matched could be placed in the pocket chart station.

The next day, when the students were engaged in their daily Making Words time, the teacher told them that the cards would be available at the pocket chart station. They were excited! As I

Students practice a Making Words lesson on their own at the pocket chart work station.

watched them during work station time, one child played teacher and called out directions to the other: "You will need the letter cards *a, e, p, l,* and *n.* Listen for your directions. Use three letters and make *pen.* Now change one letter and make *pan.* Now add a letter and make *pane.* Can you make a word with all the cards? What other words can you make?" Each time the child playing teacher gave a direction, he or she put the cards in the pocket chart for the other child to check. Then they switched and the child playing teacher became the student. Later, they took the word cards and sorted them according to rhyming patterns. All this had been demonstrated in class. This was a successful activity for independent practice because the students knew exactly what to do. It was interesting because it was a new thing to do at this center. In a few weeks, the teacher would need to change the activity again to keep the work station fresh and interesting. But all she had to do was to add another thing she'd been using during instruction. She didn't need to go out to the teacher supply store and buy a game, or try to make up a game of her own. If she wanted to add a game to spark interest, she could add one that they'd played as a class, or she could ask the students what they might like to play. Students can help us do the work—if we let them!

In a kindergarten class I worked with, the teacher complained that the ABC station was no longer working. She said the kids seemed bored with it. I asked her if I could meet with the class and talk about this station. She agreed. Before meeting with the kids, I asked a few of them to show me the ABC station and what they could do there. The first child showed me several alphabet puzzles on an unlabeled shelf and said you could put the pieces together. Another child showed me a different unlabeled shelf with a tub of alphabet games in it. It was clear to me that the students weren't even sure where the ABC station was.

When I met with the class, I showed them the tub of ABC activities. Then I pulled out one item at a time and asked what they did with it. I began with some shape cards for matching upper- and lower-case letters. It was in an unlabeled plastic zip-lock bag that was open. Several loose pieces were lying in the bottom of the tub. I showed these to the children and asked them what to do with them. They told me these belonged in the bag, so I put them there. Then I suggested to the students that they zip the bag when they finished so the pieces wouldn't fall out. I found another zip-lock bag with another set of puzzle pieces in it. Again, there were loose pieces in the bottom of the ABC tub. I showed these to the class. "Put them in the bag and zip it up so they don't fall out again," they said. We did so and returned that set to the tub. Then I found an ABC "Go Fish" card game in a broken box. "It needs its own bag," said a child. "You're right," I told him. "That way we can keep all the cards together in their own place." When we were done going through the container, the children knew what they could choose from, where to find it, and how to put things away there. I suggested to the teacher that she add one new thing to the tub as she taught. She decided to add the class's new sight words by writing each word on an index card and putting the cards on a ring. Then she'd put magnetic letters out so the children could make each word. The new ABC station was a success.

Finding the Time

The last question teachers usually ask me is "I think this will work and I want to do it, but how can I make it all fit into my already crammed schedule?" My answer is twofold: you may have to get rid of some old things to make room for the new; and you may have to multi-task. Whenever we bring home a new piece of clothing, we need to make room for it in our closet. If we keep buying and never throw anything away, we will soon run out of space. Our daily schedules are just like that. If we keep adding new routines but don't do away with something old, we'll run out of time in our day.

Look honestly at your lesson plan book. Put a star beside each thing your students did last week that truly helped them become better readers or writers. Don't mark things you *hoped* would help them. Mark things that you know worked because you saw a high level of engagement, interest, and motivation. Now look at the unmarked items. What could you get rid of? Or what could you change to make the unmarked activity more engaging, interesting, and motivating? Perhaps it could be integrated into literacy work stations as a practice activity. An activity you used to do as a whole group might be moved into work stations for students to do with partners.

After you've gone through your daily schedule, carve out a block of time for literacy work stations. In first and second grade, you'll need an hour or so. You'll need five to ten minutes daily for the mini-lesson, about thirty to forty-five minutes for literacy work station time, and another five to ten minutes for sharing time. In kindergarten, you'll need about thirty to forty minutes total. Many kindergarten teachers also have a second "center" time for traditional kindergarten centers, such as block building, housekeeping, and sand table, as well as the option to revisit literacy work stations. (See Chapter 9 for ideas on adding literacy to these traditional centers.)

Try your new schedule daily for several weeks. If you have literacy stations only once a week, students won't get good at them. They need to have clear, predictable routines in order to learn. Establishing literacy work stations is one of the best things you can do to engage your students in meaningful, independent practice that will help them become better readers and writers.

Reflection and Dialogue

Consider the following:

1. Think about what literacy work stations should look like, sound like, and feel like in your classroom. Be as specific as possible. You might brainstorm with a group of colleagues who teach your grade. Then brainstorm with your class. Share your class's list with your colleagues. What did the students come up with that you hadn't thought about? How did this exercise help you? How did it help your students?

2. Plan several mini-lessons for your work stations with a colleague. Think about everything that kids might possibly not do right, and include those things in your mini-lesson. That way students will know exactly what you expect. You might videotape a mini-lesson and share it with teachers from your grade level. Discuss how this mini-lesson helped your students.

3. Choose a literacy work station from your classroom that you've had trouble with. Brainstorm with a colleague what to do to improve the work station.

4. With a colleague, develop a plan for behavior at a literacy work station. Let students know exactly what will happen if they don't follow the rules. On a weekly basis, meet with your colleague to discuss your plan until the children's behavior is well established. Readjust your plan as needed.

5. Create a management board and a place to store work station products. Go on a "field trip" to other teachers' rooms to see their management boards and storage ideas.

Classroom Library

Two children are nestled into pillows on a colorful rug in the classroom library savoring books that the teacher has read aloud to them previously. Soft music plays in the background. Their class has been doing an author study of Cynthia Rylant, and her books are stored in a tub labeled "Books by Cynthia Rylant." Her photo is on a poster in the classroom library, and phrases the children have come up with to describe her work are displayed:

Things We Know About Cynthia Rylant

- She likes to write about her family.

- She writes about her son and her dog in the *Henry and Mudge* books.

- Many of her characters are people she really knew in real life.

- In *Tulip Sees America* she writes about her own life when she moved across the country.

- She uses lots of descriptive words so you can picture in your mind what she's saying.

"Keyonda, listen to this part. The farms in Iowa. They are pictures: White houses. Red roofs. Green, green rolling hills and black garden soil all around them. I love Cynthia Rylant, don't you? I can see her stories in my mind when I read."

"I'm reading one of her books, too—*Henry and Mudge*. They are my favorites. Do you want to read one with me?"

This is the kind of dialogue that takes place in an effective classroom library during literacy work station time. Children are reading books the teacher has read to them during read-aloud. Or they may be reading books that classmates have recommended during sharing time. The students know how to engage in discussion about books because their teacher has modeled this for them during read-aloud. They know how to choose books for independent reading, because this has also been modeled many times. They read like writers, pulling out wonderful language that they might use in their daily writing, because their teacher has also shown them how to do this.

Cynthia Rylant poster displayed in the classroom library.

What the Children Do

The classroom library is a place where students are expected to browse books and read or "pretend read." Here also, children may share favorite books or special parts of books with each other. It isn't necessarily a silent area; rather, it's a spot where children read and talk about books. You should see your students engaging in the following types of activities at the classroom library:

■ *Reading information from an "author study poster" created by the class.* As described at the beginning of this chapter, students should use what they know about authors they're studying to read and understand books in the classroom library. They might even add to the chart if they discover something else about the author as they read more of his or her books, which are stored in a container labeled with that author's name.

■ *Using a "How to Choose a Book" chart to choose books.* The teacher creates this chart with the children to help them select "just right" books for reading independently.

■ *Reading familiar books.* These are books either read aloud several times or books children have listened to on tape at the listening station that they can now read on their own. Rereading these books will increase students' reading fluency.

■ *Reading independent-level texts.* With the teacher's guidance, children should learn to choose books they can read independently. This is a critical step, enabling students to feel successful and to avoid interrupting the teacher who is reading with a small group for guided reading.

■ *Looking at pictures in a book and telling the story (in kindergarten and early first grade).* Emergent readers need to learn how to look at the pictures and tell a story or talk about the pictures in order to develop oral language, which is an important prerequisite to reading and writing. The teacher should model this important beginning reading strategy.

■ *Sharing favorite parts of books with a partner.* Children should be encouraged to talk about books as well as read them. Their talk will develop their oral language as well as provide a framework for thinking about books. Their conversation will serve as a foundation for writing responses to books, which they

Two children read a book together in the classroom library.

A child writes a personal connection on a sticky note.

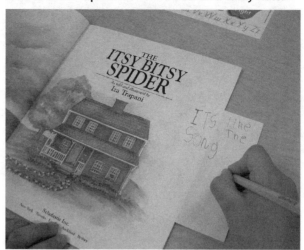

will also be asked to do in the classroom library.

- *Reading books and magazines to stuffed animals.* Young children love an audience for their reading, and stuffed animals are patient listeners. Show children how to use stuffed animals appropriately in the library as "reading buddies," not as toys to play with there.

- *Writing a response to a book.* After talking about their books, students should sometimes write responses to what they read. Sticky notes and response forms on clipboards should be kept in the classroom library to provide easy access to materials needed for writing about books.

- *Writing a book review of a classroom library book.* Students will enjoy reading each other's book reviews, which are written to encourage classmates to read the books the writers have read. Reviews are much more interesting to kids than book reports, which are often written to prove to teachers that they have read a certain book.

- *Writing a note to a friend about a classroom library book.* Provide nice paper for students to use to write a note to a friend about a book they enjoyed. Beautiful stationery sometimes motivates reluctant writers. Sometimes just putting a sticky note on a book that says "Loved this book!" with one's initials after it is enough to get someone else to read a book.

- *Writing personal connections or questions on sticky notes as a student reads a classroom library book.* After you model for students how good readers think about what a book reminds them of, children will want to write their own personal connections. Show them how to put sticky notes in the book so the edge sticks out and doesn't cover up any of the words. Other readers will enjoy reading both the classroom library books and their friends' thoughts written on notes in the books.

- *Recording the name of a book read at the classroom library in an individual reading log.* Noting books read helps readers be accountable for their reading at the classroom library. Let them carry their reading log in their literacy work station folder. (See the section "Folders and Finished Work Boxes" in Chapter 2 for more on folders.)

■ *Putting materials back in labeled containers when finished reading.* Children should be taught how to clean up when leaving the classroom library so that it may remain a pleasant place to enjoy reading and talking about books.

Reading and Talking About Books

The classroom library is not a silent place, but it should be a calm one. Children reading at about the second-grade reading level should be expected to read silently, but children at earlier stages of reading will need to read aloud softly to monitor their reading and understand what they read. Children should be encouraged to use different voices and read with expression while reading conversation. They might want to read a book with a friend, each taking the part of different characters. Quiet conversation should also take place in the classroom library. Some children may be telling the stories shown by the pictures or sharing a favorite part with a classmate.

Writing

Writing may also take place in the classroom library. This shows students the connections between reading and writing. Teachers should model ways to respond in writing to books and then provide opportunities for children to share their responses with each other.

For example, children in second grade and up may be interested in writing online book reviews. Show them how to go to www.amazon.com or www.barnesandnoble.com and click on the title of a favorite or familiar book. A screen will be displayed with information about the title. Then click on "Customer reviews" and help them read some of the reviews written there. Next, click on "Write an online review" and model how to write a brief book review. Students can write their own reviews and post them online for others to read. This will increase their reading and writing activity. They can

choose from one to five stars to rate the book and can also receive feedback from others as to whether their review was helpful or not. This is twenty-first-century literacy at its best! (See Appendix B for a sheet where students can write their online book review before publishing it on the Internet.) Some school districts also have sites for posting online reviews. You might check this out through your local district or through a search for "student book reviews" using a search engine such as www.metacrawler.com or www.google.com.

It is important that students understand that they should stay in the classroom library during their assigned time there. This will make work station time run more smoothly. Be sure that all materials needed are in the classroom library so children don't need to interrupt you or run around the classroom.

How to Set Up the Classroom Library

Take a lesson from the bookstores of the world as you establish a space for your classroom library. Think about what entices you to take a book from the shelves and read it (or better yet, buy it and take it home!). Teachers are in the same business as bookstores: we need to be selling books to kids! Today's children have many more choices for entertainment than we did when we were growing up. The twenty-first-century child goes home and chooses from TV, the computer, video games, and movies on DVD, or is involved in after-school activities or even day care. Teachers must provide quality time and opportunity for children to read during the day. Literacy work stations provide an extra chance for reading at school. So let's take a lesson from those bookstores . . .

You enter the bookstore. The space is inviting—roomy and well lit. Soft music plays in the background. Perhaps some plants give life to the space. Comfortable chairs invite you to sit down and look

Books are organized into labeled tubs.

through a book. The books are arranged by topic, by author, by genre. Many are facing outward, their covers displayed, inviting you to look closer at them. All these ideas can be applied to the classroom library.

In some schools, teachers expand their classroom library to encompass several areas in the room, or they may share a space with another teacher. They may have a nonfiction section in one part of the room and fiction in another. Or they may place tubs of books in every center and in the guided reading area for children to choose from. The most important thing is to provide books in an organized fashion to help students be able to find the material they need for independent reading.

Materials

A well-designed classroom library may include the following materials:

- A sign clearly labeling the space (or spaces).

- Sturdy bookshelves (one may be designated for fiction and another for nonfiction) to store books and help define the space.

- An open-faced book rack for displaying books with covers facing out.

- A wide variety of books and other print materials, including a balance of fiction, nonfiction, magazines, newspapers, menus, charts, and student-made books.

- Books and poems representing the cultures of all the students in the class.

- Small baskets or containers that hold sorted books and are labeled by the students.

- Comfortable seating (beanbag chairs, a futon, and/or large pillows).

- A silk plant (to enliven the space).

- A lamp.

- A rug.

- A tape recorder (for playing soft music).

- Stuffed animals for children to read to.

- Book reviews written by the class and by individual students.

- Posters made by the class on authors, how to choose books, how to write a book review . . .

- A book checkout system.

- Forms and paper with pencils attached on clipboards for writing responses and book reviews.

- Bookmarks.

- "How to Choose a Book" chart made by the class.

- "How to Write a Book Review" chart made by the class.

- Sticky notes.

- "Our Favorite Books" album.

Use the checklist in Appendix B to see if you have all the materials you need to set up your classroom library.

At the beginning of the school year, establish the idea of the classroom library with your students. Take your class on a "field trip" to the school library. Before going there, set the purpose and ask children to observe the way the school library is set up. When you get to the library, talk about the signs and labels you see there, such as "Fiction" and "Nonfiction." Show students such things as how all the books about whales are together, how all the books by a certain author are together, and how the biography section contains stories of people's lives.

When you return to the classroom, sit in a circle and have the kids share what they noticed on the trip. Discuss how the books were organized and some of the names of the categories. Then tell the students that you're going to use what you learned at the school library to set up your classroom library. Place a big pile of books on the floor. Have the class sort the books into two piles, fiction and nonfiction. Show them how to look inside each book and think aloud about how to tell what kind of book each is. For example, "This book is fiction because it has talking animals. It must be made up since animals can't talk. But this book is nonfiction.

It's about real and true stuff. It has photographs taken by a camera."

Pass out a book to two children at a time. Ask them to look at the book together and determine if it's fiction or nonfiction. Then go around the circle, have the pairs tell which kind of book theirs is, and have them put it into the appropriate pile. This may take several class periods to accomplish. Store the books in labeled boxes each day.

After the books are sorted into fiction and nonfiction, work together to sort the nonfiction books into smaller groups. Children will come up with their own ideas, such as weather books, animal books, poetry books, and people books. Share a pen with the children and write the name of each category on an index card. Then let student volunteers type these words onto the computer to make labels. Have kids add illustrations to the labels, put the labels on clear plastic shoe boxes or magazine boxes, and store the containers on bookshelves labeled "Nonfiction."

Likewise, sort the fiction books into groups with the children. These may be sorted by author, genre, easy-to-read, chapter books, little books, leveled books, etc. Like the nonfiction, the fiction should go into containers that are labeled and stored on shelves labeled "Fiction."

First graders sort books into fiction and nonfiction piles for the classroom library.

Children read alone or with partners to decide if books are fiction or nonfiction.

This activity can be done with first graders the very first week of school. It will help them begin to learn about genres and get acquainted with the books in the collection. Once, while sorting books in a second grade, I saw several struggling readers just sitting and reading instead of sorting the books. It was as though it was the first time they'd ever found a book in the classroom library that they could read! This activity also helps children develop ownership of the classroom library, which will help them to keep this space neater.

How to Introduce the Classroom Library

After setting up the classroom library with students, there are still many things that must be modeled in order for this work station to be effective. When introducing the classroom library, gather your class there and talk about what they might do at the library. Be clear and explicit in your expectations. For example, you might say, "At the classroom library, I expect you to be reading books and magazines. Choose your book quickly. Use the poster to help you. Be sure to spend most of your time reading while you're here. You might want to read to a stuffed animal. When you're finished reading, you might write a response. I should see you reading or writing the whole time you're in this area. If I see you not reading or writing, you'll have to leave and sit by me. This time is for you to practice reading and writing. Use your time well."

Then ask two children to show what this behavior would look like. Have the rest of the class observe and tell what they noticed. They will say things like, "I like the way Jasmine and Nick picked books quickly. They used the 'How to Choose a Book' chart. I saw them reading the whole time. They weren't hitting each other with stuffed animals. They did a good job of practicing reading."

What the Teacher Needs to Model

Here are some routines to model to help your students get the most from their time at the classroom library:

How to choose a book. Model often for children how to choose a book. When you go to the school library, talk about how they might choose library books. Show them how to look at the covers and consider whether they're interested in the topic. Show students how to look at the first page and try to read the words. Tell them that they should be able to read most of the words in the book they choose. Older students can use the "five-finger" test, putting up one finger for each hard word. If they find more than five words on one page, the book may be too hard and they should choose a different book.

When you take your class to the school library, remind them how to choose books. "I chose this book because I liked the picture on the cover. Inside it looked funny, and I like funny stories. I tried to read the words and could read most of them on the first page." As kids line up to leave the library, ask them to tell why they chose the book they did. This will reinforce that we should think before we choose books.

Model book choice when you read aloud to students. Tell them why you chose the book you're reading to them. Before I read aloud one day in science class, I told the children how I chose our new book: "I knew you wanted to learn more about skyscrapers and how they are built after our science lesson yesterday. So I went to the public library and looked up skyscrapers on the computer. Then I found the shelves where they keep the books about skyscrapers. I found these three books to share with you. I chose them because the pictures and captions answer the questions you had about how skyscrapers are built. When you choose books in the classroom library today, think about what you're interested in and look for that kind of book. Be sure to pick a book where you can read most of the words. Use the pictures and captions to help you, too." Be explicit in telling kids how to use what you've just modeled in their own reading.

Suggest to children that they might choose books that they know well. These might be books you have read aloud to them in class. Or they may read books from "book bags"—zip-lock bags that hold books they read in small groups during guided reading. You might keep a tub of books labeled "Our Favorite Read-Aloud Books" that they can use as a no-fail measure for choosing familiar books.

Post a list of ways to choose a book in the classroom library. Write this interactively with your class and remind children to use the information when they are choosing a book. Here's what such a list might look like.

How to Choose a Book

- Choose an author you like.

- Choose a book the teacher read aloud.

- Choose a book in a series you are reading.

- Look at the picture on the cover. Read the title. Does it look interesting?

- Look at the first page. Try to read the words. Is it too easy? Too hard? Just right?

- Look another page in the book. Can you read most of the words?

- Use the five-finger test. Put up a finger for each hard word. If you have more than five fingers up on the first page, the book is probably too hard.

- Choose a book with the level of the books you read in your reading group.

How to read or "pretend read" a book. Show children what you expect of them as reading behavior. Have them practice with you as a large group during a block of time for independent reading, perhaps for ten or fifteen minutes at the beginning of kindergarten and first grade. Talk about what you expect to see during this time. They should be reading the words if they are able to. For emergent readers, show them how to turn the pages from front to back and move left to right on the pages. Model how to tell the story by looking at the pictures. Tell them that this is how everyone reads when first learning to read.

How to talk about a book. Young children need to be shown how to talk about the books they read. Some have had many opportunities to do this at home as parents read aloud and talked with them. Others have not had this experience and need to see this modeled at school. As you read a book aloud, do so interactively. Allow children to ask questions about what you've read or to tell what it reminds them of. Stop periodically and ask them to turn to a neighbor and tell what they're thinking about. Then let a few children tell the class what they're thinking. Keep the pace moving, though, since young children won't sit for too long! This talk about books will help them learn how readers have conversations about what they read.

How to put a book away. Show children how to put books away when they are finished reading them. Some teachers like to put removable colored dots on the upper-right-hand corner of each book and a matching sticker on the labeled tub so students can easily put books away. This can solve many problems with keeping the library neat and organized.

Explain that when books are placed with the covers facing front it makes it much easier for the next reader to choose a book quickly and to have more reading time. Books put in the wrong tubs or put away upside down or backward wastes others' time.

You might have a container labeled "Book Hospital" for books needing repair that children come across while reading. This will encourage them to be careful with books. The teacher might have several student helpers or parent volunteers to mend books with tape or a stapler.

How to write in a reading log. I keep a personal reading log that lists books I've read. I show it to students to demonstrate what good readers do. If students write down titles of books they have read, teachers can keep better track of their students' reading. Show children how to neatly copy the title of the book they have read and the author's name. (Allow only books they have finished to be recorded!) Explain that noting the author's name can give them another way to think about what to read next. Many readers like to read books by the same author.

A reading log can help children set and keep track of reading goals. For example, as an adult reader I set the goal of finishing one book a month. Some second graders may set a goal of finishing two chapter books a week independently. See Appendix B for a goal-setting sheet and a sample reading log.

How to write a book response or book review. Model for children many ways to write a response to literature. After you read a book aloud, write as a class about a favorite part or parts. Eplain how the purpose of this writing is to tell others about the book so they'll want to read it, too. Provide space in the classroom library (on a wall or the back of a bookshelf) where responses can be posted and read by others. See Appendix B for sample reading response forms.

How to Solve Problems That May Arise

One of the most common errors I see teachers make in the classroom library is that they put too many books out too fast. Young children can't keep up with too many books. Of course, the library can

First-grade classroom library at the start of the school year.

also get messy when there are too many books for students to take care of. If you start with fewer books and gradually add to the library throughout the year, management and cleanup will be easier.

If children are having trouble choosing a book, reteach how to choose a book. Take a few minutes before literacy work station time to do a brief minilesson on book choice. One first-grade teacher modeled it this way: "Yesterday I noticed that some of you were having trouble finding a book. In fact, somebody used the whole time at the classroom library trying to choose a book. She looked at one book and then another until she finally just sat there and didn't do anything at all. How is this time helping her become a better reader?"

The children responded with, "If you practice reading when you're at the classroom library, you get to be a better reader. If you're having trouble finding a book, use the chart to help you. Or get your partner to help you. Or just get your book bag."

Finally, the child who'd had trouble finding the book the day before said, "It won't happen again. I know how to find a book now. And I can always read the books we made as a class because I know how to read all those books!"

When given a supportive environment and the opportunity to do so, children often can solve their own problems. We just need to open the door for them! Talk with the students daily for a few minutes before and after work station time, and help them fix what went wrong at the work stations. Take the time to re-model what they need help with.

If children aren't putting books away properly, assign a classroom helper called the "classroom librarian" to check and be sure all is well. This child's job might include checking to be sure the colored dots match up and that the books are placed back in the tubs with the front covers facing up. This student might also be in charge of book checkout for take-home reading.

Finally, you might create a classroom chart of what behavior should look like and sound like in the classroom library. See the sample below. Post this chart in the classroom library if the children need to be reminded about your expectations for this center.

The Classroom Library

Looks Like:

Kids are reading.

If kids don't know the words, they are using the pictures to tell the story.

Kids spend some time reading one book before getting another one.

Kids talk about the books they read.

Kids write about the books they read.

Sounds Like:

Quiet voices reading.

Reading a good part to someone else in the classroom library.

"This is a great book. You might want to read it, too."

"This is my favorite part."

Another possibility is to brainstorm an "I Can" list with the students that includes the kinds of things you should see at this work station. Be sure to write it with the children. Here are some things children might do at the classroom library:

I Can . . .

- Read a "just right" book.

- Read a book by telling about the pictures.

- Read a book from read-aloud.

- Tell my partner about a book I like.

- Write a book review about a book I just read.

- Write a response to a book I just read.

Differentiating at This Work Station

Think about the children in your classroom who are reading at many different levels and who have varied interests. Be sure to provide for their particular needs at the library. One way to have differentiation at the classroom library is by including several containers with leveled books. You can use Irene Fountas and Gay Su Pinnell's *Guided Reading* and/or *Matching Books to Readers* for suggested classroom or Reading Recovery® levels. Simply label some tubs with levels matching your classroom levels. You don't need to level every book in your library, but several tubs with levels marked will provide some surefire "just right" reading for children in your class, because they'll be able to turn to tubs of books at their reading level.

Leveled books in the classroom library aid beginning readers in book selection.

Reminding children that they can take their book bags with them to the classroom library to read will also insure that they are reading books at their appropriate level. Their book bags should include independent-level reading materials that they can read on their own with 95 to 100 percent accuracy with good fluency and good comprehension.

Allow children to write at their own level at this work station, too. Post models of book reviews written by your class that show students samples of quality writing for their grade level. Give them opportunities to share their responses after work station time to encourage them to keep reading and writing.

Ways to Keep This Station Going Throughout the Year

"How do I keep interest going in the classroom library all year long?" is often a question teachers ask. The easiest way to do this is periodically to change the books in this area. As you read new books aloud, have children help you decide which tub to add them to. But as you add books, remember to take some away, too, or the library may become too crowded for the children to manage. When deciding which books to take out of the library, think about the following:

■ What are my students' current reading levels? (By midyear some of the books may have become much easier than kids need for reading practice.)

■ It's spring. Should I take out all the winter books? (Not if children are still enjoying them!)

■ Does a colleague have some books he or she will swap with me to keep my collection fresh? (If the books in the library are your own, stamp your name inside of them and keep a list of what you loaned out.)

"Our Favorite Books" poster in the classroom library.

Another way to add some spark is to use your open-faced book rack to highlight a different child's favorite books every two weeks. I got this idea from visiting a local video store. Simply put a sign on the rack that says "Billy's Picks of the Week" and let that child select all the books that will be put on the rack for that two-week period. Watch the interest in the classroom library soar, especially for that student!

Another idea is to create an "Our Favorite Books" chart. As a class, name some favorites from the classroom library and then put a big chart on the wall nearby listing those books. As children read in the classroom library, have them use a sticky note to write their name on it and post it below that title on the chart.

How to Assess/Keep Kids Accountable

Remember that time spent at work stations is practice time, and you should not grade everything that your students practice. However, children do need to be held accountable for what they're doing at the classroom library to be sure they are using their time wisely and that they are truly practicing reading and writing. Here are some ideas for insuring accountability at the classroom library:

■ Observe two children a day in the classroom library. Jot down notes on a clipboard or a sticky note so you don't forget what you saw them doing. Were the children reading when you glanced at the classroom library today? Use the Classroom Library Assessment Form at the end of Appendix B.

■ Look at the children's reading logs. Have them record the date the book was read and write L beside the title to show that they read it while in the classroom library.

■ Give children opportunities to share for a few minutes after work station time. If they were in the classroom library, have them talk briefly about a book they read and/or a reading strategy they used while reading there. For example, "Today at the classroom library, I got stuck on the word *monster* and went back and read the sentence again and used the picture to figure it out." This provides a model for other children of what they might also do.

■ If you're using a favorite books chart, did the child vote for a favorite book?

■ If you use book response forms, evaluate a written response every few weeks. Let children know what you expect. For example, "I will give you a grade for your book responses. I expect you to do a book response once every two weeks. Use the sample hanging in the classroom library to help you."

■ Do the children ask you to add a book to the classroom library after you've read it aloud? Are they talking more about the books they've read?

Reflection and Dialogue

Consider the following:

1. Is your classroom library inviting to readers? What could you do to make your library more appealing? Ask students for suggestions.
2. How are the books organized in your classroom library? Develop a plan to improve the setup of your library.
3. What do you need more of in your classroom library—fiction, nonfiction, magazines, other print materials, shelving? Take an inventory.
4. What would you like to add to your classroom library—writing materials? an author study? Ask a colleague for suggestions. Use the checklist in Appendix B.
5. Observe your students at the classroom library. How independently do they work there? What could you model to help children read more effectively on their own?

4

Big Book Work Station

Two students stand in front of the Big Book easel. One is using a pointer and the other is preparing to turn the page. As one child points to the large words in the book, the two read together with expression. They sound just like the characters in the book. When they come to the end of a page, they laugh at the funny part and then quickly move to the next page. You can see and hear their joy as they read. These children are working in tandem, helping each other fix errors and keeping meaning flowing as they read together. When they finish the last page, they say, "Let's read it again!" They exchange places as the pointer and page turner and repeat the reading of this favorite Big Book.

Later, the teacher spies them "playing teacher," asking each other to find certain words and kinds of words in the Big Book. One student says, "Find the word *can*. Put some highlighter tape on it. Good job! Now find a word that rhymes with *can*." The other child searches for those words and reads them. The children are doing exactly what their teacher did with the class the previous week as they read this book together in shared reading.

The Big Book work station is usually one of the most successful stations in the classroom. The amount of time the teacher takes to model how to read Big Books has a direct effect on the quality of the reading practice that children do at this work station. The more the teacher models with Big

Two children read a familiar Big Book at the Big Book work station.

Books during shared reading, the more successful students are as they practice reading on their own. The clearer and more explicit the teacher, the more children take on reading strategies as their own.

What the Children Do

The Big Book work station is a place where students practice reading and rereading familiar texts previously taught during shared reading. The reading is fluent because these are books students can read easily. Basically, the children do whatever they saw the teacher do with Big Books during instruction time.

You should see the following types of activities at the Big Book work station:

- *Pointing to words (one-to-one matching) at emergent reading levels.* Having emergent readers use pointers to one-to-one match words is very valuable. It helps children pay attention to print and notice how print works. It helps them develop a concept of what a word is (as compared to a letter).

- *Reading in phrases at early to transitional reading levels.* To help children become more fluent in their reading, have them practice reading Big Books with lines of text printed as phrases. Model how to read across the line of print with your eyes and encourage children to do the same with a partner. They might use a pointer to run under the line of print as a phrase.

- *Using reading strategies modeled during shared reading.* Shared reading is one of the best opportunities for a teacher to model what good readers do. For example, if you show how good readers use pictures to help them think about the story and make this strategy explicit, your students will be inclined to do the same thing as they practice reading. You

may even hear them use the language of the teacher: "Good readers use the pictures to think about the story and what the words might say." You should see students practice whatever you modeled during shared reading of Big Books.

- *Reading a nonfiction Big Book and finding important information.* As you read nonfiction Big Books with the class, show them how to find information you need and how to do this quickly. Model how to use the index, the glossary, and the table of contents as well as how to find specific information they might be wondering about.

- *Talking about favorite parts of Big Books.* Expect to hear students talking about what they liked in a Big Book. You might have them find a favorite part to read to the class during sharing time after work station time.

- *Reading a fiction Big Book with character voices.* Students practice what was modeled during shared reading. Books with several characters are excellent for teaching children to read with fluency and expression. Sometimes children might want to choose character parts; at other times they simply read together, changing their voices to sound like the characters.

- *Writing a book review of a Big Book.* If you show students how to write a book review during shared writing, you can suggest that children write a book review of a Big Book to encourage others to read it. Post these reviews near the Big Book station. You might even keep a three-ring notebook to store student-written book reviews of Big Books.

- *Writing personal connections or questions on sticky notes as a student reads a Big Book.* Many teachers are finding that if they model how to write what a Big Book reminds them of during reading and jot this on a sticky note with their initials, children will follow suit. Children enjoy reading these sticky notes as well as the Big Book text.

- *Acting out a Big Book with a partner.* Drama can aid comprehension. By supplying simple props you've modeled with during shared reading, students can enjoy retelling a book, thereby improving both oral language and understanding. You might occasionally have children "perform" a Big Book during sharing time.

- *Finding words you know in a Big Book.* To add an element of word study, have beginning readers find high-frequency words in a familiar Big Book. Provide them with highlighter tape or a masking device so that they can mark these words and practice reading them.

- *Finding certain kinds of words in a Big Book.* Have students find three-letter words, compound words, or rhyming words in familiar text and mark these words with highlighter tape. You might have them occasionally write the words on a list. Use the task cards in Appendix C.

- *Matching words in a Big Book.* Make a set of words you want children to become more familiar with from a Big Book, such as high-frequency words or color words. This will

High-frequency words from the story are written on sticky notes for children to match to words in the book.

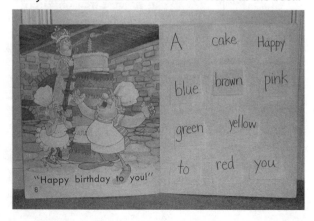

encourage emergent readers to pay closer attention to print. Write each word on a sticky note and place them in the back of the book. Then have children search for those words and place the sticky notes below or on top of the corresponding words in the Big Book.

- *Substituting words using sticky notes in a Big Book.* Provide children with blank sticky notes and show them how to write a word that could be substituted for a common word in a Big Book. For example, a child might change *said* to *shouted.* Then have children go back and reread the book with the new words.

Selecting Big Books for Shared Reading

Big Books should be chosen carefully for use during shared reading before being placed in the Big Book work station. You might think about choosing a book that:

- Is at a reading level slightly above the guided reading level of most students in your class.

- Can be enjoyed through multiple readings.

- Has text large enough for all students to see during shared reading.

- Has rhythm, rhyme, and/or repetition, especially at emergent and early levels.

- Can easily be dramatized.

- Is about a topic of high interest to your students.

- Contains high-frequency words you want your students to learn.

- Has spelling patterns your class is studying.

- Contains interesting words and language.

- Introduces your students to a new genre.

Remember to include both fiction and nonfiction Big Books during shared reading and then place them at the Big Book station. Shared reading is your opportunity to scaffold the class's reading of a whole text for the purpose of teaching students reading strategies—what good readers do as they read. It should be an enjoyable reading experience for all. Every child in the class should feel successful as you introduce a Big Book and then read it with the children several days in a row. Each time you read, you can focus on another aspect of reading and thinking. The children's experience in shared reading will directly affect their practice at the Big Book work station.

Writing

Both reading and writing can be practiced at the Big Book station. Again, the children's success in writing here hinges directly on the teaching that precedes their independent practice. While you read a Big Book with the children, you might do a think-aloud, modeling your personal connections to the book. Ellin Keene and Susan Zimmermann have written extensively about this process in *Mosaic of Thought* (1997). Stephanie Harvey's and Anne Goudvis's *Strategies That Work* (2000) is another practical resource for modeling comprehension strategies and incorporating writing, as is Debbie Miller's *Reading with Meaning* (2002). For example, you might say something like this while reading *Cats, Cats, Cats* by Joy Cowley (1995):

> When I read that page, it reminded me of when my daughter was little and wanted a cat. It's all she could think about. That thought helps me understand this story better because I know how the author is feeling. She is longing for a cat. I'm going to write that on this sticky note so I can remember what I was thinking here— "like Jessica longing for a cat"—then I'll put my initials, D.D., so others know whose connection this is. Now when you read this book at

Personal connections are written on sticky notes and placed in the Big Book for others to read.

the Big Book station, you can read the story and the sticky notes! I'll put some blank sticky notes there for you to use, too. You can write what the book reminds you of when you read. It will help you to remember and understand the story better.

Children eventually love to have writing tasks at the Big Book station. It must be carefully modeled, however, so children know exactly what is expected—and what is not allowed. It is probably best to include writing at the Big Book station only when you are sure children will not write directly in the books (it's usually safe by around late kindergarten or early first grade).

How to Set Up the Big Book Work Station

The Big Book work station is one of the easiest to set up because you only need the materials you teach with, such as Big Books, an easel, and a pointer. You'll probably want to set up this station in your large-group teaching area, since that is where you will be teaching with the materials first. If you are right-handed, place a chair on the left side of the easel so that you don't reach across the words and block them as you read the book with the children.

Have all your materials organized and at your fingertips to make for more efficient teaching. Some Big Book easels have a tray built into the bottom, which provides a handy storage space for a caddy filled with small pointers, highlighter tape, sticky notes, pencils, and dry-erase markers. You might also have a small dry-erase board at this station for on-the-spot demonstrations of how words work as you read.

Post a large ABC chart and a chart with the children's names written in large print by the Big Book station. These resources can be used during shared reading to help children problem-solve new words. If you model with these charts, children will use them during independent practice time, too. For

example, if the class is reading together and stumbles over the word *theater,* you can direct their attention to the names chart and say, "This word starts just like Theo's name. Let's start the word and think what would make sense." Use the ABC chart to help children learn beginning sounds, too. Over time, other charts, such as a vowels chart or a rime chart, might replace the ABC chart. The names chart may be used all year. Last names might be added to it. Highlighter tape can be placed over sounds the class is learning, such as *oy* in *Roy.*

Provide a place for storage of Big Books, to keep them in good condition. Some Big Book easels have built-in storage for the books. One inexpensive storage option is a large laundry basket placed to the right of your Big Book easel. (The Hip-Hugger laundry basket by Rubbermaid® is just the right size for this.) Label the container with the Big Book work station sign. On the right-hand side of the basket attach two small plastic sink containers (the kind

A names chart is posted by the Big Books container, which is made from a laundry basket.

Reading and writing tools are stored on the side of the Big Books container.

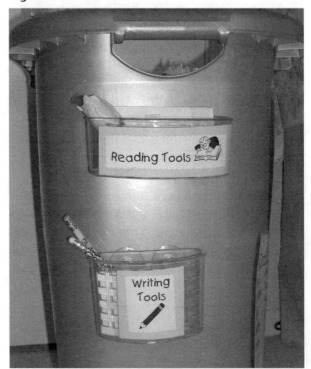

that hold kitchen sponges) with suction cups and label these "Reading Tools" and "Writing Tools." You can then place your highlighter tape, small pointers, and masking devices in the Reading Tools container. Put a pack of sticky notes and two pencils in the Writing Tools holder.

Materials

Materials you might include at the Big Book work station include:

- Familiar Big Books (fiction and nonfiction).

- Class-made Big Books.

- A Big Book easel.

- A Big Book storage container.

- Highlighter tape.

- Masking devices.

- A chart of children's names.

- An ABC chart.

- Props for dramatizing stories.

A complete Big Books work station has all materials centrally located.

- A sturdy container with several short pointers in it.

- A pretend magnifying glass (for finding words).

- A small bubble wand (for finding letters).

A word about Big Book easels: be sure the children can see the print on the page when they're sitting on the floor during shared reading.

Create your own Big Books as a class if you don't have many Big Books in your school. An excellent resource for this is *Think Big! Creating Big Books with Children* by Cynthia L. Johnson (1998).

Ideas for Big Book Pointers

Children enjoy using pointers as they read at the Big Book work station. Pointers are most useful for emergent readers. These beginners need to point to every word to develop one-to-one matching and to learn to pay attention to print. Once children are paying attention to print, they should be encouraged to read without the pointer. They might use the pointer to point just to the line they are reading instead of to each word. Or they can use the pointer to read by phrases and to point out end punctuation to remind themselves to stop. Keep the pointers simple so they don't interfere with the reading! There are many inexpensive items that can be used for pointers:

- Chopsticks.

- Unsharpened pencils.

- Old wooden spoons.

- Rulers.

- Pick-up sticks.

- Old car antennae.

- Magic wands.

Big Book pointers made from dowel rods, car antennae, and a swizzle stick.

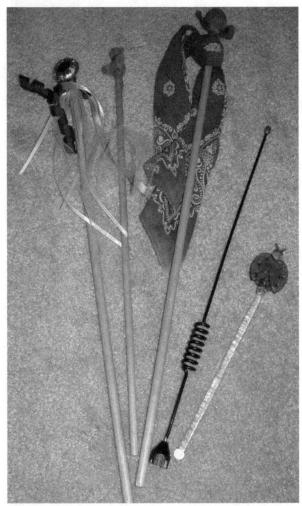

- Telescoping wands.

- Toothbrushes.

- Plastic flowers (single stems).

- Small items from floral picks glued onto floral wire.

- Halloween fingernails.

- Small finger puppets.

- Dowel rods (cut in half to make them shorter) with small erasers or other objects glued to the

end with epoxy glue from a hardware store. (It's best to glue these at home, as the fumes are strong.)

How to Introduce the Big Book Work Station

The Big Book work station is an easy one to introduce for students if you've done shared reading with them. The most important thing is to place books that your students can read successfully at this station. Tell the class that you have been reading Big Books together since school began, and now you're going to let them read the books on their own. Tell them that their job is to practice reading and rereading Big Books here and to do the things you showed them during shared reading.

You might make an "I Can" list with them, such as the following:

I Can . . .

- Read a Big Book with my partner.

- Find words I know and put highlighter tape on them.

- Read the words with highlighter tape on them.

- Point to the words (or the lines) as I read.

- Write my connections on sticky notes.

Remind children that the books must be used very carefully. Review how to turn the pages and how to use pointers. Be explicit about what you expect and why. For example, you could say something like this:

You know how to turn the pages. We practiced this during shared reading. Many of you have had the job as the page turner while we read Big Books together. Remember to turn the pages carefully so they don't tear. That way the books will last for a long, long time and we can all enjoy them. Pointers are to be used *only* for pointing to the Big Book pages. If anyone plays around with the pointers, they will have to leave the work station. There will be no warnings. I know you know how to use the materials. Have fun reading here with your partner.

What the Teacher Needs to Model

The more explicit your modeling, the more successful students will be at the Big Book work station. Model the following during mini-lessons:

How to turn the pages. See the section above for specific language to use when teaching children how to carefully turn the pages of Big Books. Let children practice this by taking turns as the "page turner" during shared reading. Show them how to use their thumb and pointer finger to "pinch" the page at the top corner and carefully turn it. If you have wooden pegs on the Big Book easel ledge, you might want to remove these to prevent torn pages.

How to use a pointer. Show children how to use a pointer. Tell emergent readers to make the words match. Be sure they point crisply from one word to the next. Don't let them slide the pointer under the words.

After children have mastered one-to-one matching of words, show them how to use the pointer to read phrases. Have students gently slide the pointer under phrases of words to encourage more fluent reading.

Remind children that pointers are used only for pointing to words and phrases. Short pointers, such as wooden dowel rods cut in half, tend to be used more for pointing and less for sword fighting. Tell students that if they play with the pointers, they won't be able to use them.

How to use highlighter tape. Introduce highlighter tape during shared reading. Show students how to use it to cover words they know. Students love how the words show through the transparent colored tape. Always have them read the words they highlight. At the Big Book station, you might also have them copy some of their highlighted words onto paper. Later, ask them to read their list of words to you.

Be sure to show students how to remove the highlighter tape from the Big Book after they have finished reading it. The highlighter tape may become permanently attached if left in a Big Book too long. Show them how to stick the reusable tape into a file folder or onto laminated index cards at the station for the next children to use.

How to use sticky notes. Model the use of sticky notes during shared reading. Show children how to cover up a difficult word before reading the book and then guessing it during the reading by gradually peeling back the sticky note, one or two letters at a time.

Show students how to use sticky notes to make connections (for first and second grade only). Model how to initial the note to show who wrote it and show how to stick the note on the page so it doesn't cover up any of the words or important parts of the pictures.

How to choose a Big Book and read it together. Remind children how to choose a familiar Big Book they can read together. Tell them to help each other with the tricky parts. One student might be the pointer and the other the page turner. After reading a Big Book once, they might switch roles and read it again. Or they could both point and read it together. Model different ways students can read Big Books together.

How to put a Big Book on the easel before reading it. When you read a new Big Book during shared reading, show students how to carefully place it on the Big Book easel. You might draw a line in the middle of the ledge that holds the Big Book to show how to center the book so it doesn't slide off while reading. This makes it easy for children to line up the middle of a Big Book on the easel.

How to return books to the Big Book container. Teach children how to store Big Books after they finish reading them. Be sure they know exactly where to put the Big Books, such as in slots with the spines showing in the back of the Big Book easel or in a laundry basket labeled for Big Book storage. Careful storage of Big Books protects them and extends their use.

How to use props for retelling. Clearly model how to use props so students don't misbehave with them during work station time. Practice many times with the materials during shared reading before moving the props to the Big Book station for independent practice. See the section on "Adding Props for Drama" in this chapter for more ideas.

How to write at the Big Book station. During shared reading, model the use of writing on sticky notes. Post a sample book review in the Big Book work station showing how to write a review for Big Books read during shared writing. You might keep these reviews in a notebook and encourage children to add their own book reviews to the collection. See the section on "Writing" in this chapter for more ideas on writing at the Big Book station.

Reading for Fluency

Because children enjoy reading Big Books over and over again, this station is ideal for helping children develop reading fluency. To encourage fluent reading, choose books that have one or more of the following elements:

- Repeated lines.

- Rhyme and rhythm.

Highlighting devices made from highlighter tape, a bubble wand, and a fly swatter with a hole cut out.

- Dialogue.

- Lines written as phrases.

- Question and answer format.

- Familiar story lines.

- Familiar oral language structures.

While reading these Big Books instructionally, remind children to "read so it sounds like talking." Tell them to "read this part quickly" or "put it all together so it sounds like you're saying it to someone." Suggest that students read parts and pretend they're really in that situation. If you notice that children aren't pausing or stopping at punctuation, it's sometimes helpful to have them highlight periods with transparent highlighter tape before reading as a reminder to stop at those marks.

Using Big Book Task Cards

Task cards help focus word study (and letter study) during students' time at the Big Book work station.

Children use Big Book task cards for word study.

Be sure to demonstrate with these cards during shared reading before having children use them at the work station. It is best to introduce just one new task at a time to insure success for all. Following the initial reading of a Big Book, you might use a task card to help children focus on a particular type of word or letter. For example, you might say "Find a word that ends in a vowel" and then have students take turns coming to the Big Book and highlighting words that end in vowels. It is very important that children *read* these words as well as mark them in the book! Emphasize the process of "find the word and read it" so children will do the same thing when they work independently. All of the task cards can be hole-punched in the upper-left-hand corner and put on a ring. Be sure to add only one new card at a time to the shared reading task card ring. Continue to use the cards during shared reading as well as at the Big Book station. Sample task cards can be found in Appendix C.

Adding Props for Drama

Many simple props can be added to the Big Book station to encourage retelling and improve children's comprehension and their reading with expression. Be sure to keep the props uncomplicated and easy to manage, both to save your time and to help the children stay focused. Teach with these props during shared reading so students know how to use them correctly.

Have children practice retelling stories with you. If you skip this important step, you may wind up with children acting silly or misbehaving at the work station. Here are some suggestions for props:

■ Copies of characters glued onto tongue depressors.

■ Plastic name-tag holders with names of story characters printed on a tag inside each.

■ A simple piece of clothing that represents each character (such as a plastic crown for a queen, or a measuring cup and wooden spoon for the bakers in *The Birthday Cake* by Joy Cowley).

■ A small plastic toy that represents each character (such as a frog, cat, dog, and pig for a book on farm animals).

■ Paper plate masks with large holes cut out for the eyes and mouth with a tongue depressor for a handle.

Students use masks while rereading and acting out a Big Book.

How to Solve Problems That May Arise

Potential problems in the Big Book station usually relate to managing materials. For example, the books may tear if they are not used properly. It is important to show children how to turn a page carefully by pinching the top corner of the page with two fingers and gently turning it. Let students who may be having trouble with this take turns being a page turner during shared reading to practice with your guidance. Likewise, have children read the Big Book by placing it on the easel instead of the floor. There is less opportunity for damage from someone inadvertently stepping on a Big Book when it is on an easel. However, some oversized Big Books may work better on the floor. Be sure you have plenty of space for children so they will be less likely to crowd the book and rip it. Also, check your Big Book easel. If it has small pegs for holding open pages, you might want to remove these to prevent the pages from tearing.

A teacher I was working with told me she was having trouble with pointers in the Big Book station. Her students had broken many of the pointers. When I asked how this happened, she said it happened when a substitute was in her classroom. Be sure children know how you expect them to use materials both when you are in the classroom with them and when you are not there! If you don't think your students can handle working at stations independently yet, have a substitute do something else with them in your absence.

Differentiating at This Work Station

The best way to differentiate at the Big Book work station is to provide a variety of Big Books your class

A class-made Big Book.

has read together. Keep some old favorites on hand, so students can easily find something familiar that they can read. You might also put a colored dot on the front of the easiest to read Big Books to lead struggling readers to books you know they can read successfully.

Having some class-made Big Books is a way to insure that even the most struggling reader has something to read. Student-made books often encourage even the most reluctant reader to give it a go! Use a digital camera to snap pictures of your students and their classroom activities. Then create Big Books around these photos.

The use of task cards can also provide differentiation. Let children pick the card they want. For example, the open-ended task "Find a word you know you know" allows every child to be successful. One child might point to and read *I* while another student locates and reads *stop* on the same page. Another option is to print task cards on different-colored card stock. Use one color for easier tasks and another color for more advanced ones, and then guide students to practice with the color best matched to their needs.

Ways to Keep This Station Going Throughout the Year

Novelty will guarantee student interest in the Big Book work station over time. Here are some ways to provide novelty at this station:

- Put a new Big Book in the station.

- Add a class-made Big Book.

- Add a new pointer.

- Change the color of the highlighter tape.

- Add a new or different shared reading task card.

- Change the child's partner.

- Add props for retelling a story in a Big Book.

- Add sticky notes and pencils for writing connections and questions related to the Big Book.

- Add sticky notes with words from the book for matching to the Big Book.

- Add blank sticky notes for students to write synonyms for or substitutions of words in a Big Book.

- Add masking devices such as colored sticky notes.

- Change the color of the blank sticky notes.

How to Assess/Keep Kids Accountable

If you have done a good job of modeling during shared reading, children will usually stay on task at the Big Book work station. If they can easily read and really enjoy the Big Books at this station, students will generally behave. Beyond this, some

other ways to keep students accountable at the Big Book station include the following:

- Periodically, invite two children to perform the reading of a Big Book during sharing time. This will give others the message that their reading and rereading is important practice and has an audience.

- Have children initial the sticky notes that they use at the Big Book work station. Collect these over time and look at the quality of children's written interactions with text.

- Include a "Things We Learned from Reading This Big Book" chart clipped to the back of a Big Book. Encourage children to list what they learned and initial their writing. Look at their responses.

- You might teach children how to tape-record their reading at the Big Book work station and let them listen to it. Teach them to read the title of the book and say, "Read by . . . and . . ." Use this for assessment, too.

- Use the forms in Appendix C to assess students at this station. Quickly jot down reading behaviors you notice. Share with children what you observed.

Reflection and Dialogue

Consider the following:

1. Do children easily and joyfully read Big Books at this station? What could you do to increase the quality of students' reading and writing at this station?
2. Are students reading with fluency and good expression? What could you model to help them improve in these areas?
3. How are the Big Books organized in your classroom and in your school? Do you have a way

of storing Big Books in your room that protects them? Can you easily find Big Books your students can read in the school library?

4. Do you currently have a variety of Big Books available? Count the number of fiction and nonfiction Big Books you have for children to reread. Plan for a balance.

5. Plan to make a Big Book with your class. Share ideas and final products with a colleague.

6. Observe your students at the Big Book work station. What are their favorite activities there? Share with a colleague.

5

Writing Work Station

Two students sit side by side at a table near the word wall. Each is writing a message. One is making a card for a friend who is absent; the other is writing a letter to the teacher about something he did at school today. The children are surrounded by print at this work station. All the tools they need as writers are right at their fingertips: charts of writing done with the teacher and the class, beginning dictionaries and word books, a chart of children's names, and a handwriting strip showing how to form letters correctly.

"How do you spell *you*?" one child asks the other.

"It's on the word wall," replies his partner. "It's that tricky one that starts with *y*, not *w*. Mrs. Diller wrote it in the Morning Message today." They look at the word wall together. After finding what he was looking for, the child copies the word *you* onto his paper.

These children are developing a system for helping themselves become better writers. They are creating meaningful messages at this work station that will be shared with others. When they have finished writing, they place their cards and letters into individual mailboxes for other students and the teacher. This kind of writing that receives an immediate response will do much to further their desire to write.

Place the writing work station near the word wall.

In another classroom two children have finished a piece of writing during their daily writing workshop time, and they plan to type their pieces on the computer during their turn at the writing work station later in the day. In their room, the teacher has set up the writing work station right beside the computers so students have easy access to them while they write. Their teacher takes them to the computer lab weekly, too, so they know how to use the keyboard and how to save their work. Lots of modeling in this classroom has paid off: the children are productive when they work at the writing station during independent work time.

What the Children Do

A wide variety of writing activities should be presented at the writing work station throughout the year. The following might be included:

■ *Writing something—a list, a card, a letter, a story, a fact book, a survey . . .* Teachers should provide many models of how to compose various forms first and then post samples in the writing station to help children remember what these forms of writing look like.

Display samples of writing forms in the writing work station.

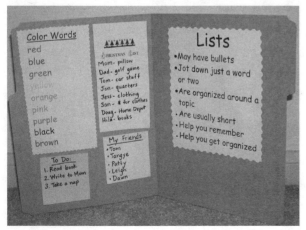

■ *Talking about your ideas for writing; tell a partner what you're thinking about writing.* Students can use the writing help board for ideas. See the section "Ideas for the Help Board" later in this chapter for ideas on how to set up the board.

■ *Writing a description—of something I see in the room, of a classmate, of my pet, of my mom, of my teacher . . .* Children are often better at writing about the here and now than writing about things that have happened in the past. Letting them write about real things that they can see, hear, touch, smell, and taste may prompt them to produce more writing.

■ *Telling a friend a story.* Talk is a very important part of writing. It helps us rehearse our ideas. Have children use the writing help board to come up with ideas and tell each other stories. It usually works best when the teacher has modeled how to tell personal stories about things that have really happened and has given children opportunities to tell their own stories in front of the class.

■ *Writing down the story you told.* Writing a story helps children remember what they want to say and allows them to share it in a permanent way with others.

■ *Doing "expert writing."* All children are experts at something. They usually have a topic they are passionate about. For some children, it's dinosaurs; for others, it's butterflies or spiders. Some love Barbie dolls or computer games. Encourage children to write about what they know—and care—about. Let them write several pieces on the same topic that might eventually be stapled into a "chapter book."

■ *Helping someone revise and edit.* Children can put into practice what you have taught about revision and editing. A simple checklist made with the class could be posted here as a reminder.

- *Practicing correct letter formation.* Writing from left to right and from top to bottom aids fluency. Beginning writers can practice writing their names and high-frequency words with special materials in this writing work station.

- *Writing messages others can easily read and understand.* Make writing for real purposes and real audiences the focus at this station. Children will produce better writing when they care about their messages.

- *Beginning to use reference materials, such as word walls, dictionaries, and thesauri.* Working with a buddy to use reference books makes this task easier. Model how to use these materials in class and then provide several copies at the writing station for students to use for practice.

- *Working on pieces from writing workshop.* Children should be allowed to take their writing folders to this work station so that they can continue working on pieces begun in writing workshop. Time in the writing work station gives them more time to develop their writing, especially with the support of a partner.

- *Playing with creative ideas.* Some children enjoy using story starters, such as pictures in magazines, to come up with their own fictional pieces. Others prefer writing research reports. Let children have the freedom to choose their topics at this station, but provide aids for those who want them.

- *Using books read aloud as models for writing.* Display some of the books you've read aloud in class, particularly ones you've used as examples of good writing. Books used in author study might also be displayed near the writing station for students to use as references if they get stuck. Be sure to use both fiction and nonfiction as models for writing and encourage students to write about real, true things as well as things they have made up.

Set up the writing work station near the computers to integrate the two.

- *Using the computer for writing.* If your classroom has a computer, teach students how to use simple writing programs, such as Kid Pix or Storybook Weaver. Many second graders like to do simple revising and editing on the computer; they find that these tasks are easier to do with the help of technology.

How to Set Up the Writing Work Station

Think about providing "helps" for writing as you set up the writing work station. Placing the work station near the word wall is a great idea, if you can find a way to do so. It allows children easy access to words you want them to practice spelling correctly.

A small table is helpful, too, as it provides a hard, smooth surface for writing. Place a few chairs around the table to invite conversation and writing help from peers. Of course, your goal is for your students to become independent writers, but there's much to be said for the role of writing communities in helping writers grow. Be sure to model conversation about writing throughout the day, so children will learn how to talk like writers about their work.

Provide a table and chairs to create a comfortable writing space.

Label stacking trays and drawers to organize types of paper for writing.

Use stacking trays for storing paper. Put a different kind of paper in each tray and add a label to each to help the area stay neat and organized. Likewise, place writing implements in labeled containers. The writing work station can easily turn into a mess, but with thoughtful planning and good teaching it can remain orderly. You needn't have a large amount of materials out at once, since only a few children will be working at the writing station at a time. The fewer the items, the easier the cleanup!

If you'd like, place some sort of mailbox in the writing station to encourage children to write notes to each other. Such notes are a fine example of meaningful writing for a real audience. You might use an actual mailbox purchased from a hardware store. Alternatively, some teachers use a small piece of furniture divided into cubbies. A good, inexpensive way to create mailboxes is to get clear plastic pocket lingerie bags from a dollar store and put a three-by-five-inch index card with a child's name in large black letters into each pocket. A single lingerie bag usually contains twelve pockets, so two of these should be enough for most primary classrooms. Hang these in the writing station and you have instant mailboxes.

If possible, position your writing station near a computer, if you have one in your classroom. This will encourage students to compose and edit on the computer, thus helping them learn another real-life skill as they practice writing. Be sure to give young children clear instruction on how to keyboard, how to create documents, and how to save files as needed. Revising and editing are much easier for students when they can use a computer to help them accomplish these tasks.

For very young children, I like to include a large dry-erase easel for writing on a vertical surface. This aids large muscle development, which young writers need before they move to the more complex, fine muscle movement necessary for writing. In addition, writing on a large vertical surface seems to encourage children to form the letters more fully, from top to bottom. I have also found that reluctant writers often love the fluid, forgiving surface of a dry-erase board. They can erase without getting holes in their paper!

Clipboards are another welcome addition in the writing work station. Many students in pre-K and kindergarten are at the self-selected copying stage—that is, they like to walk around the room and copy words from their environment. By doing so, they learn about print and how it works. Even if they can't read all the words back to you, they are exploring print—*if* they do this on their own. Never force a child to walk around and copy print, especially if the child is already writing and using sound-symbol correspondence.

A help board is another good thing to have in the writing area. If you decide to make one, use a large project board, the kind used for science fairs. With the children, add "helps" over time to remind them of what they can try as writers.

Ideas for the Help Board

A help board is a resource children can use to help them solve their writing dilemmas so they don't need to disturb you, the teacher. The key is to teach with this board first so students know how to access the information recorded on it. Here are some ideas for what to put on a help board:

For pre-K and kindergarten

- Ideas for what to write about (use labels and photos or magazine pictures).

- Forms of writing introduced (label, list, letter, book, chart, poem, research, description, story, survey, note . . .).

- Ideas of where to go for help (word wall, ABC chart, names chart . . .).

For first grade

- Ideas of what to write about (use labels and photos or magazine pictures).

- Forms of writing introduced (label, list, letter, book, description, autobiography, poem, story, research, book review, instructions, recipe, informational text . . .).

- Ideas of where to go for help (word wall, ABC chart, names chart, peer conference, picture dictionary . . .).

Help boards for kindergarten, first grade, and second grade.

- Author study information (tub of books by one author studied with information about that author to remind students of how good writers write).

For second grade

- Ideas of what to write about (use labels and photos or magazine pictures).

- Forms of writing introduced (list, letter, book, poem, book review, instructions, recipe, description, informational text, interview, realistic fiction, folk tale, biography, rules, newspaper article . . .).

- Ideas of where to go for help (word wall, names chart using first and last names, peer conferencing, beginning dictionary, word study notebook, writers' notebook . . .).

- Author study information (tub of books by one author studied with information about that author to remind students of how good writers write).

Materials

Remember not to put out too much in the writing work station, at least to begin with. What follows is a list of what might be used in the writing work station in the course of the entire school year. Here are possible materials for this work station:

- A help board, as described above.

- A variety of paper (white, colored, unlined, lined, decorated, plain . . .).

- Labeled stacking trays (for paper storage).

- A variety of writing implements.

- Labeled containers for writing tools (pens, pencils, crayons, etc.).

- Alphabet strips with correct letter formation noted on them (for handwriting help).

- An alphabet chart (for spelling help).

- A names chart (for spelling help).

- Simple word books (for writing ideas and spelling help).

- Picture dictionaries and other beginning dictionaries.

- A beginning thesaurus.

- Samples of high-quality student writing.

- Samples of a variety of forms of writing, labeled (list, letter, poem, card, invitation, book review, research, survey, instructions . . .).

- Blank books (white paper folded and stapled).

- Blank cards (construction paper folded in half).

- Staplers and tape.

- Charts made by the teacher and students together intended as aids to student writers (what to write about, how to spell a word, what good writers do . . .).

- Real objects to describe (live flowers, insects, rocks, toys . . .).

Materials include writing utensils, a variety of paper, an "I Can" list, and letter writing helps.

- A magnifying glass (to aid in observation).

- Magazine photos.

- Envelopes.

- Theme words on rings.

- A dry-erase board (especially for pre-K and kindergarten).

- Author study tubs.

- A basket or tub labeled "Finished Work."

How to Introduce the Writing Work Station

Starting small is always a good idea when introducing a work station. Begin by talking with children about where writers get their ideas for writing. Model how you get your ideas. Start a help board by posting the following sign: "I can write about . . ." Tell the children some of the things you could write about and add those ideas to the board. For example, write "me" and "my family" and "my friends." Add photos or magazine pictures to go with each entry. Then model for children how to write about one of these topics. Show students how they can use the help board to help them write. Then put the board into the writing work station along with some basic materials, such as paper, pencils, and crayons.

Be explicit about what you want the children to do at this work station. Tell them directly that they must write something. One year I realized that most of our first graders were going to the writing station and drawing, but not writing. I had to tell them what I expected. Children are free to use pictures in their writing, but they need to focus on becoming better writers. You should expect them to write at this work station and let them know that this is what you expect.

Suggest to students that they use the help board to decide what to write about. Over time, introduce forms of writing children might use. At this point, add the sign "I can write a . . ." to the help board. Begin with something simple, like a list. Add the word *list* to the board and make a list with the children. Post the list you have created on the help board as a model. If you do lots of list writing in class with the children, you'll see this kind of writing at the work station, too. Of course, you should allow children to write stories or notes or anything else they're interested in writing. Stay away from prescribed prompts that everyone has to use. Allow children to choose topics and forms at the writing work station and you'll probably see better writing. Over time, introduce new forms of writing and add samples to the help board.

What the Teacher Needs to Model

The writing work station will be most successful if the teacher has modeled the following routines over time. Many models, not just one, are needed for children to do their best.

How to get an idea for writing. Show children how you get your ideas for writing. Think aloud with them while using the writing help board. Say, "What shall I write about today? Hmm, I could write about the leaky shower and its drip, drip, drip. But that might not be very interesting to you. Or I could write about my dog, Hercules, and the gigantic hole I found that he dug in the backyard. That's on our idea list on the writing help board: writing about my pets. Would you like me to write that story? I think it would make you laugh." After writing the story, remind children again to look at the help board for an idea if they get stuck with what to write about.

How to spell a word you're not sure about. Again, model this while you're writing in front of the students. Show them how to write the sounds they hear. Demonstrate how to use the word wall for help. Also, show them how they can circle a word that still doesn't look right with a yellow or other brightly colored crayon and return to work on it later.

How to use materials properly. When you add new materials to the work station, especially things like tape or a stapler, be sure to show children exactly how you expect them to use it. You may need to limit the number of staples used for a book or the length of the tape students may use.

How to put materials away. Teach children specific routines, such as how to put the cap on a dry-erase marker and listen for the click. Show children how to sort paper stored in the stacking tray. Have children help you make labels for containers to be sure things get returned to their proper places. When students help you make the labels, they will feel more ownership of the space and are more likely to keep "their" writing work station tidy.

How to mail a letter. When you introduce classroom mailboxes, teach children how to put the name of the person they are writing to on an envelope. Show them how to sign their name and use only kind words in the note or letter. Then demonstrate the procedure for how letters will be delivered. Decide whether you will have a mailperson deliver the mail or whether you will allow children to check their mailboxes at a certain time of the day.

How to confer with a peer. Teaching children how to handle conferences will take a great deal of practice and patience. See *Teaching the Youngest Writers* by Marcia Freeman (1998) for some good ideas on conferences.

What to do with finished work. Set up a labeled basket in the work station for finished writing. Or direct children to put their finished pieces in their folders from writing workshop. Or children may place their pieces into their work station folder. Just be sure to have a procedure so children know exactly what to do with their finished writing.

How to use a word book. As you write in front of the class during modeled writing, show children how to use a simple word book. One of my favorites is *My First Word Board Book* by Angela Wilkes (1997). Show children the page "All About Me" and point out how all the body parts have words beside them. Tell them these are called labels. Then show how you could draw a picture of yourself and write labels using the book. On another day use the same page and show how you could use the labels to write about yourself. Tell students, "I could use these words to help me write about what my face looks like. I could write that I have blue eyes. The word *eye* is right here beside the girl's eye, so that would help me know how to spell that kind of *eye*." After you show children how to use a word book, place it in the writing work station and watch them do just what you modeled!

How to use a dictionary. Children who see their teacher using a dictionary to model how to look up words will be more able to use this tool themselves.

Provide dictionaries and model their use.

Show children how to write a word with temporary spelling, stretching it out and writing down the sounds they hear. Then tell them, "I'm not sure I spelled it right so I'll circle it with a yellow crayon as a signal to go back and fix it later. When I'm finished writing, I'll use a dictionary to help me. To use the dictionary I must use the first sound in the word, which I usually know. I keep looking until I find the word; then I check my spelling. If you have trouble, get your partner to help you with the dictionary."

Writing Work Station Possibilities

Here are some ideas for the writing work station for kindergarten, first grade, and second grade.

Kindergarten

Purposes:

- Practice correct letter formation.

- Use letter-sound correspondence in writing.

- Write a message.

Materials:

- Letter formation materials (letter tracing cards, tactile letters, rainbow letters . . .).

- ABC chart.

- Names chart.

- Simple word book.

- Paper.

- Pencils and crayons.

Possible "I Can" list (brainstorm ideas with students):

I can . . .

- Practice writing my name correctly.

- Write my friends' names correctly.

- Make a card.

- Write words from the word book.

- Write a note to a friend.

Assessment and evaluation ideas:

- Observe letter formation.

- Can you read the children's writing?

- Look at their cards and notes.

- Have them share their writing with the class.

First Grade

Purposes:

- Write a message to communicate to someone.

- Talk with a peer about your writing.

Materials:

- Paper.

- Pencils and markers.

- Construction paper.

- Prestapled blank books.

- Magazine pictures.

Possible "I Can" list (brainstorm ideas with students):

I can . . .

- Make something and write about it.

- Write a letter to a friend.

- Make one book about something I know about.

- Write about a magazine picture.

- Talk with my partner about my writing.

- Read my writing to my partner.

What to teach in mini-lessons:

■ How to talk with a peer about your writing.

■ How to talk in a quiet voice.

■ How to use markers (and other materials) properly.

■ How to write a book.

Assessment and evaluation ideas:

■ Observe student conferences.

■ Can you read the students' writing? Does it contain good ideas? Is it organized?

■ Look at the students' books and letters.

■ Have students share their writing with the class.

■ Have students tell about their conferences and how they helped each other with their writing.

Second Grade

Purposes:

■ Include good leads.

■ Write a letter to thank or invite.

■ Write a nonfiction book about what we're studying in science.

■ Use capitalization and punctuation correctly to make messages readable.

Materials:

■ Pens, pencils, and crayons.

■ Paper.

■ Envelopes.

■ Stickers.

■ Author study tubs—examples: nonfiction authors Melvin Berger and Joanna Cole.

■ Model of a letter.

■ Tub of quality nonfiction books on the science topic being studied, written at an easy level for most second graders.

■ Models of class-made nonfiction books on previously studied topics.

■ List of good leads (previously developed with students).

■ Reminder list of what to capitalize (previously developed with students).

■ Reminder list of how to punctuate with periods and question marks (previously developed with students).

Possible "I Can" list (brainstorm ideas with students):

I can . . .

■ Write a nonfiction book to inform.

■ Write like an author we've studied.

■ Write a letter to a friend to invite them to or thank them for something.

■ Use a good lead in my writing.

■ Use capital letters for names and at the beginning of sentences.

■ Read my writing and listen for stops so I can put periods and question marks where they belong.

Assessment and evaluation ideas:

■ Look at the students' stories and letters. Use a rubric that evaluates whether the pieces contain the following elements: a specific purpose and audience; a good lead; correct use of capital letters; correct use of end punctuation.

■ Have students share their writing with the class.

How to Solve Problems That May Arise

The writing work station works most smoothly in classrooms where regularly scheduled writing time takes place daily. Students who are used to writing understand what good writers do and can do these things independently. They know how to choose their own topics, put their ideas on paper, spell words they are unsure about, and read their writing to a friend for help and feedback. They know how to do these routines because their teacher has repeatedly modeled these things for them. For help with setting up a daily approach to writing, you might read *Writing Workshop: The Essential Guide* by Ralph Fletcher and JoAnn Portalupi (2001). The writing work station can be difficult if you haven't modeled well or set explicit expectations. Without these, children may do sloppy work or no writing at all at the writing work station. The key to success is good modeling so that students will know exactly what you want them to do. Writing aids in the work station will also help children to do their best.

You might place samples of good writing in the work station to show children what this looks like. You might also place a sample of poor work with the universal "no" sign on it. (Use a sample from a child who has moved away, and remove the name. Or make one up yourself.) Visuals help children know what you expect.

Another problem that sometimes arises in the writing work station relates to materials. Children can waste lots of time sharpening pencils, for example, so have a can of sharpened pencils available and don't allow children to sharpen pencils during writing time. Also, sometimes students use up too much of a material too quickly. Your prestapled books may all be used up by a single child, for example, before anyone else has a chance to get to the station. To prevent this from happening, put out just a few at a time. Limit students to only one

Display samples of good- and poor-quality writing to set the standard.

book per visit. Post this rule in the writing station so children know your expectations.

Teachers often complain that students just don't use the materials correctly at the writing station. To avoid this, show children clearly how to use markers and stamps if you want children to use such materials in the writing work station. One teacher introduced stamps during interactive writing. As the teacher and students composed a message together, they "shared the pen." The teacher wrote some of the message and the children wrote some. Instead of having the students use a pen, the teacher had them stamp some of the words. This gave her a chance to show her students how to use this new item. Then, when she placed stamps in the writing station, children knew how to use them properly. You might consider having a child serve as materials manager to monitor and replace materials at the writing work station. That way you won't be interrupted when students need paper or pencils.

Differentiating at This Work Station

Students in your classroom are probably writing at different levels at any given time during the school year. The range may be broad, from a child who is writing only the first and last sounds of a word to one who is writing dialogue. Because of this, you'll need to differentiate at the writing work station.

The best way to do this is to give children choices. When you provide models and materials and let children choose what they can do, they are more likely to be successful. For example, many different things can be done with nature magazine pictures. Emergent writers might add labels using sounds they hear; beginning writers might compose a sentence or two describing a photo; more advanced writers might use the pictures to write a poem or even a nonfiction piece.

You might occasionally want to use colored tubs to provide materials for children at different levels. For example, if you teach kindergarten and

you want some children to practice writing names for letter formation, keep a blue tub of materials just for this and tell children who need practice with that skill to use the blue tub today. Or if you have special tools for peer editing, you might require that certain students whom you've been working with on peer editing use these materials, which you've put in a different-colored tub.

Ways to Keep This Station Going Throughout the Year

Adding new touches on a regular basis will keep the writing station alive. Remember to add only one new item at a time for maximum effectiveness. Here are some ideas for keeping this station interesting:

- Change the color of the paper. Simply adding colored paper if you've had white will make the writing work station seem new again.

- Change the writing tools. Put in new decorative pencils or gel pens. Remember to put out only one or two so you can keep track of these hot items! A student assigned to be the materials manager can be a great help with this.

- Add new decorative stationery. You or your students can create new or themed stationery with computer graphics, or by using stamps or stickers.

- Use paper precut with large die cuts in various shapes.

- Add to the help board during writing instruction. A portable help board can easily be used for both large-group teaching and at the writing station.

- Add prestapled books.

- Add photos of your class, especially those taken with a digital camera (faster and less expensive to process).

- Add new word cards with seasonal or theme words on a ring. (Be sure you've taught with these words first!)

- Put mailboxes away for a while if interest wanes, then bring them out again. Everything old can seem new again.

- Add an "I'd Like Mail" sign to the station and post a few kids' names under it with a brief plea from each child for someone to write to them.

- Add a character, such as "Mrs. Bear," a large stuffed animal that writes notes to the class at night. Encourage students to write notes back to Mrs. Bear.

- Add a large piece of paper labeled "Daily News" each day and invite students to write their own news, if this is a routine you use in your classroom. Or post the Daily News in this station and encourage students to add to it.

- Add magazine pictures that might spark ideas for writing.

- Add a Magna Doodle (only if you've taught students how to use it properly) or a magic

Joy Cowley author study materials promote interest when they are used for teaching and then added to the writing work station.

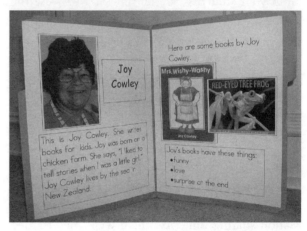

Prop bag with sample shared writing done by the class.

slate or one of the new black dry-erase boards for novelty.

- The addition of tape and/or a stapler will also generate interest. Again, teach children very carefully how and when to use these materials in the work station.

- Add new word books or dictionaries.

- Add colored envelopes or inexpensive greeting cards.

- Add writing prop bags, small gift bags containing three or four small items (e.g., a small ball, a toy dog, and a whistle) that may prompt story ideas.

- Add new author study materials.

- Add a new message board.

- Let children compose and revise on the computer.

How to Assess/Keep Kids Accountable

To keep track of students' progress, use a chart like the one in Appendix D. Adapt it to account for the particular things you've modeled and are expecting from your students. Several times a week, use the form to spot-check what children are doing at the writing work station. Eyeball a group at a time and quickly check off what you observe students doing there. Jot down notes that will help you remember specifics. Also collect student writing done at the station and look for evidence of what you've been teaching. Some of this writing can be used for taking grades since it is part of the children's independent work.

To keep children accountable at this station, let them share their writing with the class during work station sharing time. Ask them what they learned

about writing and what they learned about themselves as writers as they worked at the station. Helping children become more aware of themselves as writers will help them be more accountable. Posting samples of good and poor writing in the station will also help with accountability, as students will have something to compare their work with. Above all else, let children write about what they know and care about. Children who care about their writing do a better job overall.

Reflection and Dialogue

Consider the following:

1. Where is your writing work station located? Can children easily access the word wall from the station? Is it an inviting space that encourages children to do their best, or is it tucked away in an obscure spot where there just happened to be a shelf?

2. What can you do to make your writing work station more appealing to students? Look at the writing work stations of several colleagues, perhaps even in different grade levels. What ideas can you borrow and use to add pizzazz to your station?

3. What helps do you have available for children at the writing work station? What are they using often? What are they using well? What are they not using? What might you change as a result?

4. What do children choose to do when they come to the writing work station? Do you observe them mostly talking, writing, drawing, or a combination of these? What can you do to encourage them to do more of any of these behaviors? Do they write mostly fiction or nonfiction? Work with them to expand their writing repertoire.

5. Where do you display children's writing in your classroom? Do children help select what

"Eyeball" students to see if they are doing what you expect.

will be posted? Does everyone write about the same topic, or is a variety of writing displayed? Think about the message this gives to children about the work of writers. Talk about this with a colleague.

6. With permission, visit the classroom of another teacher when he or she is not in the room. Look for evidence of what children are writing about. Jot down what you think that teacher is teaching about writing right now. Have that teacher do the same thing in your room. Then compare notes. Discuss what you can do to better communicate what you are teaching about writing. Remember, what you saw when you visited is what parents see also.

6

Drama Work Station

The drama work station is one that changes throughout the year and looks a bit different from kindergarten through second grade. It is a wonderful place to improve reading comprehension and fluency, as well as to encourage creative expression. In a classroom of emergent readers, you might see children retelling a familiar story from a read-aloud book, using a flannel board and felt pieces (or a magnetic board and characters with magnetic tape attached to the back) to act out the story. They use the book to remember the order of events and to help them with the details of retelling. They point to pictures and match up the characters as they eagerly tell the story they know so well. As they work together, they pay attention to the meaning of the book and increase their comprehension.

In a classroom of early readers, children might use a familiar book from guided reading to retell a story with stick puppets they made. One student reads a page from a small copy of *The Farm Concert* by Joy Cowley (1995), while the other child acts out that part with the puppet characters. You hear fluent reading and animated expression. The animal puppets make occasional comments, such as a loud or soft *moo, moo,* depending on the size of the print in the book. After reading *The Farm Concert* once, the children switch places and the other child reads while his buddy acts out the book. A basket filled with zip-lock bags containing other familiar books and accompanying puppets for rereading and retelling is close at hand. Each bag contains a copy of the book and the pieces for retelling. To help with materials management, a digital photo inside each bag shows all the items that should go in the bag.

In a second-grade classroom, two students are reading and acting out a play they've written themselves. When finished with that activity, they read a reader's theater script they are familiar with from shared or guided reading. A folding board like those used in science projects defines the drama work station area and functions as a theater. Scripts are placed in clear plastic sleeves on the back of the board. These students are reading with ever-increasing fluency and expression. They ask the teacher if they can perform their new play during work station sharing time that day.

What the Children Do

Children are eager to come to the drama work station to read plays and retell books. The focus here is on reading for fluency and comprehension. The more the children read, the better they get at reading. This is also a space where oral language related to books can flourish. Children develop creative expression at this work station, too, as they enact favorite stories and plays. Activities such as the following might be included at the drama work station:

■ *Retelling a familiar book.* It is very important that only familiar books be used for retelling. Model how to retell a book first. There are different formats for retelling fiction and nonfiction because of the structures of these kinds of texts. You might use the retelling cards in Appendix E for modeling and place these in the drama station once children are familiar with them to aid in their retellings.

■ *Using puppets to retell a familiar book.* Puppets can be student-made, teacher-made, or commercially produced. Simple puppets will help children focus on the rereading and retelling. Store these in zip-lock bags or a small basket in the drama station.

■ *Using props to retell a familiar book.* Simple props, such as small plastic animals or toys, can be placed in prop boxes that accompany a favorite book. Label each box with the book title and a picture of the objects that go with it.

■ *Using dramatic pieces to retell a familiar book.* There are many ways to create dramatic pieces for retelling. The section below, listing materials for the drama work station, will suggest ways to do this.

■ *Reading a familiar play.* Plays in the drama work station should be familiar so all children can successfully read them. Read the plays together several times in shared reading. The plays could also come from guided reading. Many publishers produce plays for young readers in little-book form. Appendix E lists some sources of easy-to-read plays in reproducible form, as well as titles of books written as plays.

Retelling a favorite book with retelling cards.

Scanned figures glued to tongue depressors make puppets for retelling.

■ *Reading a reader's theater script for a familiar book.* In this activity, students read a play to an audience. Reading expression, without props, is used to convey meaning. Old basal readers may include reader's theater scripts. Students can also learn how to write a script from a short story, such as a folk or fairy tale. Appendix E lists some sources for reader's theater scripts.

■ *Reading a student-authored play.* After reading several plays together, you might write some plays with your class. Choose a very simple story to rewrite as a play, such as *The Three Little Pigs.* Children will love to read plays they and their peers have written.

■ *Creating and using character cards for reading a script.* Three-by-five-inch plain white index cards might be placed at the drama work station for children to use as character cards. Show them how they can simply copy each character's name from the script onto a card, then distribute these cards among the actors as a way to decide who will read each part. They can read the play once, then switch cards and read it again. Store the cards in a small container in the drama station.

Writing an ad for an upcoming play.

■ *Writing ads for the play students will enact.* Performing plays invites a variety of writing opportunities. Students can write ads on construction paper or dry-erase boards telling about their play. Using a science project board with a dry-erase surface provides an easy way for children to write ads with minimal materials and space requirements. You might provide theater word cards that say "Now Showing," "Now Appearing," "Next Performance," "Coming Attractions," "Starring," and so on to help with spelling.

Students use character cards to decide who will read which part.

Students perform a familiar play and practice fluent reading.

■ *Audiotaping a performance.* Adding a tape recorder to audiotape a performance will give children a chance to hear their reading and do some self-assessment of their reading fluency. Model how to use a tape recorder. You might have a card file set up with a ten-minute tape labeled for each child. Teach children how to record and save their work.

How to Set Up the Drama Work Station

You don't need a fancy puppet theater to create a drama work station. An easy, space-saving way to set up this station is to use a science project board. It can be folded and tucked into a corner for storage when it's not work station time. A project board with a dry-erase surface on one side (available at many office supply stores) gives you a built-in area for writing ads. You can also use a large flannel or magnetic board to create an area for retelling. Provide labeled containers for materials, such as props, puppets, books, and scripts.

Start small. Put out one familiar story and its retelling pieces or one play and its character cards. This will help children learn to manage materials as

Science project board turned into a theater.

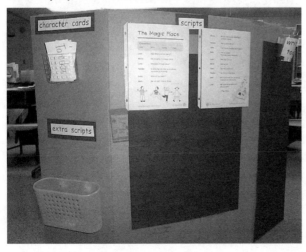

well as behavior. Add materials to this station over time as you observe children needing new stories to keep this station fresh.

Materials

Materials you might place at the drama work station include:

■ Familiar books for retelling.

■ Puppets for retelling books.

■ Flannel board and felt-backed pieces for retelling.

■ Magnetic board and magnetic-backed pieces for retelling.

■ Prop boxes.

■ A dry-erase project board or puppet theater.

■ Character cards.

■ Blank three-by-five-inch cards to be used for new character cards.

■ Markers.

■ Scripts from familiar plays.

■ Small books of plays.

■ Reader's theater scripts.

■ Containers for storing materials.

■ Tape recorder and short blank tapes for children to use for recording plays read.

How to Introduce the Drama Work Station

The best way to introduce the drama station is to decide on a focus, such as retelling familiar books or reading plays. If you choose retelling, use a book

Retelling pieces stick to carpet-to-carpet rug pad.

that you've read aloud several times and that is a favorite of the students. Pick a book that has objects or characters that can be represented by props or puppets. For example, you might choose *The Bag I'm Taking to Grandma's* by Shirley Neitzel (1995). It's the story of a child who's visiting Grandma overnight and is packing all the things he'll need. Gather together a baseball mitt, a few small toy cars, a small rocket ship, two identical plastic animals, a stuffed rabbit, a pillow, a book, a flashlight, and a bag that can hold all these items. Have two children act out the story by putting the objects into the bag as you read the book. Then show how to retell the story by using the book. Have one student hold the book and tell the story while turning page by page, while the other child puts the objects in the bag and acts it out. Let them reverse roles when finished. Then place the book and the props in the drama work station.

Gradually add books and props or puppets or flannel board pieces to the drama work station in the same way. Use charts to aid students in retelling both fiction and nonfiction pieces. Appendix E provides example of retelling cards that can be used as models for your retelling charts.

Introduce plays to readers in shared reading. Use a commercially produced play from those listed in Appendix E or from some other source. Reproduce the play onto an overhead transparency. Talk with the class about how to read a play. Show them where the title is, how the characters are listed at the top, and how they should read just what the character says and not the character's name. Read the play together once. Then divide into parts and read it again.

The next day, reread the play. This time introduce character cards. Have available a blank index card for each character in the play. Then, with the students, write the name of a character on each card. Students can help with spelling while you write the names on the cards. Next, divide the class into groups so each represents a character from the play. Hand one child in each group a character card. That's how students will know which part to read. Then read the play again.

Tell students that when they go to the drama station they can read this play on their own. Have a copy of the play printed for them at the station. Place each page into a clear plastic sleeve fastened to the back of the project board with Velcro. This frees up students' hands while they read so they can use puppets or props, if desired. Have the character cards in a zip-lock bag attached to the board, too. Tell the children to distribute the character cards and use these to read their parts.

Over time, introduce new plays and reader's theater scripts to children in a similar way. Gradually, move students toward writing their own plays and scripts to be read at the drama work station.

What the Teacher Needs to Model

The drama work station will be most successful if the teacher has modeled the following routines over time. Several models, not just one, are needed for children to do their best.

How to retell a book. Show children specifically how to retell books. Begin with a familiar book, preferably one that you've read several times in read-aloud. Folktales are good choices because they have a small number of simple characters, easy-to-remember dialogue, and repetition. Use the cards in Appendix E to give children a structure for retelling. First, retell the story for them, pointing out the elements you are including. Then move to retelling with them. Provide support as needed, but have students tell most of the story. Finally, have children take turns retelling the story alone. Ask a volunteer to retell a story to the class while you give help as appropriate. Be sure to teach how to retell both fiction and nonfiction texts.

How to use props and puppets. Adding props and puppets can add extra support, as well as fun, to the retelling and reading of plays. Show children exactly how you expect the props and puppets to be used. Talk about ways to use them appropriately. Explain what will happen if children use them in inappropriate ways (such as puppet fighting). Then tell the children that you will take action and remove them from the drama station immediately if they don't follow the rules. Limit the number of props and puppets to keep this area easier to manage. The less there is, the better the children will be able to use the materials. Keep the work station varied and interesting over time, though, by adding new puppets and props and putting away some of the old ones. You can always resurrect old favorites later, if you wish, to energize this station.

First graders learn to act out a story as a play.

Comprehension goes deeper as students reenact a familiar story.

How to read a play. Introducing plays to children is probably best done in shared reading. Read plays together, as a whole group, in Big Books or on overhead transparencies. Teach children about the specific text features of plays, such as the character box often found at the top of the page, which lists all the characters, and the way character names are written with a colon following the name to indicate who says what.

How to write a play. Use a familiar story to write your first plays together. Folktales work well for this. Examine plays you've read together in shared reading. Then be the scribe for your class as they tell you how the play should be written. Be specific in modeling how to write the character names in a box at the top and how to give the name of the character followed by a colon with that character's dialogue beside it. Explain how to include a narrator or stage directions to fill in action. After you have written

Shared writing of a play using a folktale.

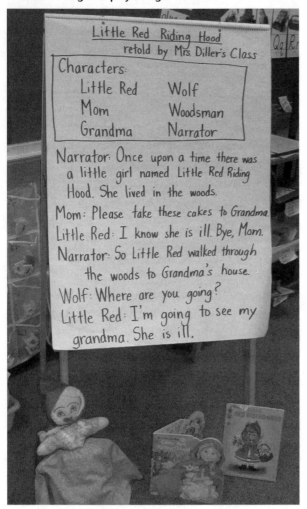

several plays together, some children will be ready to write their own plays at the writing work station. You might include in the station the plays you have written as a class as models for students to use as they write independently.

How to Solve Problems That May Arise

Most problems at the drama work station relate to behavior. If students are not familiar with a book, they may easily get off-task while here. Because it is easy for children to make up unrelated activities with props and puppets (such as puppets hitting each other on the head), it is essential that students know exactly what is expected of them at this work station. They will need many shared experiences with retelling familiar stories before they can work independently. If you notice disruptive behavior, check to be sure the stories the children are working with are familiar to them and that they understand what they are supposed to do with the materials at the work station.

The same is true of plays and scripts. Children will need to learn how to read and act out plays appropriately. With good modeling and organization of materials, most students should be successful at this work station. Be sure to keep adding new materials over time to keep interest high.

Differentiating at This Work Station

Choose books with simple story lines for retelling. Children who are more proficient readers might read the book aloud, while others can "read the pictures" to aid in retelling. The more verbal child might tell or read the story while the other student uses the puppets or props to help retell. Over time, make available books at various levels and from many genres. The variety will help meet the needs and interests of different students. Just be sure that the books used for retelling are familiar to all the children.

Provide plays and scripts with parts of varying difficulty. (Often the narrator's part is more challenging.) Help students find parts they can read easily to help them build fluency. If needed, you can put colored dots on the character cards to indicate parts that are easier to help struggling readers find appropriate material.

Ways to Keep This Station Going Throughout the Year

Variety is the key to keeping the drama work station interesting. Leave some old favorites at the station while adding new texts introduced in read-aloud, shared reading, and/or guided reading. Remember to add only one new book or script at a time to keep things novel. Here are some ideas for keeping this station interesting:

- Add a new story.
- Add a nonfiction book.
- Add new props.
- Invite students to gather props to go with a book.
- Add new puppets.
- Use student-made puppets.
- Change from a flannel board to a magnetic board or vice versa.
- Use stories with students' names and their photos on Popsicle sticks as props.
- Add a new play.
- Use a different kind of card for character cards (change the shape or color).
- Write a play together.
- Include student-made books for retelling.
- Include plays written independently by students.
- Include new published plays.
- Add new reader's theater scripts.
- Change the color of paper the plays are printed on.

How to Assess/Keep Kids Accountable

Periodically, observe students at the drama work station using the form in Appendix E. Be sure to let students know specifically what your expectations are. Creating an "I Can" list with them can be very helpful. Here are some samples of what to include on this list:

I Can . . .

- Read and retell a book.
- Use props to retell a book.
- Use puppets to retell a story.
- Read a play with a friend.
- Make and use character cards.
- Write a play.

Teachers often avoid opening a drama station because they fear it will be too noisy or disruptive, but clearly defining parameters and teaching expected behaviors will keep this from happening and will insure that students will act responsibly in this station. Here are a few additional ideas for assessment and accountability at the drama station:

- At times, invite students to perform their retelling or play for the class during work station sharing time.
- Have children occasionally record their reading of a script or their retelling of a story. Model for them how to make an audiotape that includes their names, the date, and the title followed by their reading or retelling.
- Catch children in the act of retelling and reading plays by taking a digital photo of them as they perform, then post it for others

to see. Students might even write captions for their photos and create a display in the drama station.

Reflection and Dialogue

Consider the following:

1. How do children's retellings compare with those done earlier in the year? Are children improving in retelling and comprehension throughout the year? How does their retelling of fiction compare with their retelling of non-fiction?
2. Are students reading plays and scripts with good fluency and expression? What could you model to help them improve?
3. Observe your students at the drama station. What do they choose to do most often? What do they do the least? What do you need to add or change to improve the effectiveness of this station?
4. Plan to write a play with your class using a familiar story. Share the resulting ideas and products with a colleague.
5. What are some of your favorite books you've used for retelling? Share them with your colleagues.
6. Are children behaving cooperatively at this station? If so, what have you done to foster those behaviors? If there are problems, what do you notice? Problem-solve with a colleague, if necessary.

ABC/Word Study Work Station

In September two children sit beside the magnetic chalkboard, which has been turned into an interactive word wall. Each word, including the children's names, is attached to the board with magnetic tape. A small set of shelves nearby holds word study materials. One child is putting an ABC puzzle together and singing the ABC song while she works. The other is matching magnetic letters to words printed on cards. Each word card contains a picture of a farm animal with the matching word printed beside it. The magnetic letters are sorted and stored in a fishing tackle box.

A month later, several new activities have been added. Some children still choose to do ABC puzzles, but now they are also reading ABC books. Many of these books were read aloud to the class before being placed in the ABC station. Some students are doing letter sorts, putting letters with sticks on one side of the magnetic board and letters with circles on the other. As they do this, they are learning about features of letters, or how letters are used.

By January, in the same classroom, this station looks quite different. Words have been added to the word wall, and students are sorting them. "These words have two letters: *to, is, my, me, am.* These words have three letters: *and, cat, the, Mom.*" Some

Turn your interactive word wall into an ABC/word study work station by using a magnetic surface, such as a chalkboard.

students are stamping words from the word wall onto paper and naming the letters as they do so: *"The—t, h, e—the."*

By the end of the school year, some earlier activities are still being done. However, more students are playing simple word games. The children enjoy playing Concentration or Memory using their high-frequency words printed on cards. Some read the ABC books they have made throughout the year. One child is even doing a crossword puzzle.

What the Children Do

The ABC/word study station is one that requires much differentiation throughout the school year. Within any classroom, there is a wide range of students' strengths and needs. Be sure to offer choice within this station and add to the materials frequently. However, be careful not to have too many materials here at one time or cleanup may be difficult.

Here is a list of what children might do at this station. What changes from one grade to the next is the level of difficulty of the reading, writing, and spelling tasks. See Chapter 10 for specific ways to plan for the students in your classroom.

Children sort magnetic lettes by their feature (sticks, circles, circles and sticks).

Wikki Stix form letters on a dollar store plastic place mat.

- *Sorting letters.* To help young children learn letters, have them sort them by various features, such as those that have a stick, a circle, a dot, a hump, a hook (tail), a slant. Use magnetic or foam letters at first so students can feel the shape of the letter. Then move to letters printed on cards.

- *Making letters.* Have children practice writing letters, too. As they learn to form letters, they are learning the letters' visual features. Begin with large paper on an upright easel. Provide a variety of writing tools, such as markers, crayons, and colored chalk. Students can also use Wikki Stix or play dough to make letters.

- *Doing ABC puzzles.* Use commercially produced wooden or foam puzzles to help students learn the visual features of letters and become familiar with the order of the alphabet.

- *Reading ABC books.* Provide a variety of ABC books. In kindergarten, begin with books that depict one letter, picture, and word on each page. Use more advanced ABC books as you move up the grade levels.

- *Writing ABC books.* Children enjoy making their own books. Provide blank pages or blank books. Let students add drawings or stickers to match the beginning sound on each page. You might make a class book and give children

ABC charts are good for many tasks, such as children's matching letters and pointing to each letter as they sing the alphabet.

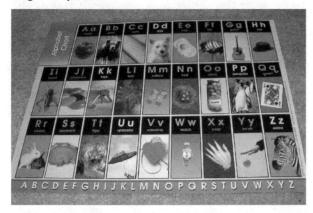

prepared pages with a letter on each for them to illustrate.

- *Reading ABC charts.* Make or use commercially produced large ABC charts with your class. Read these together in shared reading. Then provide smaller versions of these charts at the ABC/word study work station for children to practice reading. Children can also match magnetic letters to the letters on the chart and name the letters as they do so.

- *Sorting words.* To help students learn how words are put together, provide individual

Students sort words by the number of syllables on a magnetic chalkboard.

words on cards for them to sort in a variety of ways. They might sort the words by such features as number of letters, number of syllables, initial sound, ending sound, vowel pattern, or part of speech.

- *Making words.* Children can make words with magnetic letters, letter tiles, pasta letters, letter cards, Wikki Stix, and so on. This manipulation of letters teaches them how words work.

- *Illustrating words.* Children can investigate word meanings by illustrating words in books, on cards, or on a bulletin board display. Provide beginning dictionaries as models. Children might also make their own picture dictionaries.

- *Doing word hunts.* Students can look in familiar books to find words with a particular feature, such as the long *e* sound, and copy these onto word hunt sheets (see Appendix F).

- *Putting words in ABC order.* Every classroom should have a word wall arranged in alphabetical order. Children can take the words on and off the word wall as they practice learning the order of the alphabet. They can also put individual word cards into ABC order, perhaps starting with the names of their classmates.

- *Playing word games.* Many educational publishers provide a variety of word games. Commercial games, such as Boggle Jr. and

Tactile letters are used to make words.

Attaching word cards to a magnetic chalkboard creates an interactive word wall.

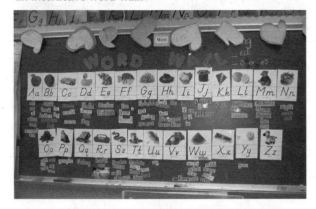

Scrabble Jr., are also available. Teacher-made games like Concentration or Memory can be used at this station, too.

■ *Doing dictionary/thesaurus work.* Students need to learn how to use a dictionary to check the spelling, meaning, and pronunciation of words. They should also become familiar with the thesaurus to help them choose better words in writing. Provide purposeful tasks for students to develop ease in using these reference books for word study.

How to Set Up an Interactive Word Wall

Word walls should be built with the students' help throughout the year to help children learn to recognize (decode) and produce (spell) words. You can use a wall, cabinets, a magnetic chalkboard, or even the space under your chalkboard for the word wall. If space is limited, you might use a tri-fold science project board. Try to place the word wall low enough for the children to be able to reach the words.

To save time, use commercial letter cards or a cut-up alphabet frieze to set up your word wall. Use both the upper- and lower-case forms of each letter. Place the cards in alphabetical order with some space under each letter where words that begin with that letter may be posted. You might start the wall with children's names at the beginning of the year. Place each student's name under its initial letter. You might include a photo of each child, too. Add words throughout the year that represent spelling patterns you are studying. Also add high-frequency words, a few at a time. For older students, include spelling "demons," words that are tricky to spell. Expect students to be able to spell word wall words correctly, and hold them accountable for spelling them correctly in their writing. When most children can spell (and read) the words correctly, remove those words from the wall. Some teachers make a little celebration out of taking a word off the wall because children have mastered it.

If possible, make your word wall interactive so students can manipulate the words on the wall. There are several ways to do this. If you have a magnetic chalkboard or dry-erase board, you might reserve part of that space for your word wall. Simply attach a small piece of magnetic tape to the back of each alphabet and word card. Some teachers use a large sheet of Velcro fabric or felt for their word wall and attach the cards with small pieces of Velcro. Others use a large sheet of construction paper for each letter, with paper clips attached through tiny slits in the paper for holding words, and the sheets attached to a wall or to cabinets. A small piece of magnetic tape is stuck to the back of each word card so the word can be removed and sorted on a metal surface, such as the side of a file cabinet or teacher's desk. Another way to make your word wall interactive is to place a library pocket under the words for each letter. For example, under the *Aa* words, a library pocket contains additional copies of the *Aa* words that appear on the word wall (*all, at, and, Abby, a*). Students can remove these words from the pocket to sort them or play other word games with them. When they have finished using the cards, they return them to the pocket.

An interactive word wall made with a poster board, each word attached by a paper clip (with a bit of magnetic tape on the back of each card) fit through a slit in the board.

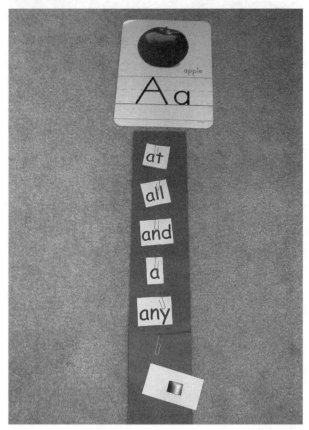

Create a magnetic space for sorting words and letters by taping off part of a magnetic chalkboard (or a file cabinet or teacher desk front).

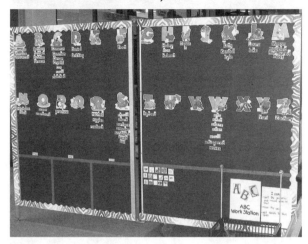

An excellent resource for learning more about word walls is Janiel Wagstaff's *Teaching Reading and Writing with Word Walls* (1999). The book contains ideas for setting up and teaching with several kinds of word walls—an ABC word wall, a chunking word wall, a high-frequency word wall, and a grammar and punctuation wall.

How to Set Up the ABC/Word Study Work Station

Placing your ABC/word study work station near the interactive word wall encourages students to work with the words you are focusing on in your class-room. If you have taught well with your word wall, students will have many activities they can already do at this station.

Along with the word wall, include an area in the work station for sorting words and letters. You might hang a small pocket chart for sorting cards. Or partition off part of a magnetic surface (a magnetic chalkboard or large dry-erase board, the metal front of your teacher desk, or the side of a file cabinet) with colored tape. Divide it into two or three spaces to create sections for students to sort different kinds of words or letters. Then provide sorting ideas written on cards, which can be posted above each section. Here are some possibilities for sorting cards:

Letter Sorts

- Stick (line).
- Circle.
- Dot.
- Hump.
- Tail (hook).
- Slant.

Poster board die-cut letters sorted by letter.

Letter formation cards made from sandpaper die-cut letters glued onto black poster board.

Word Sorts

- One letter (or two, or three, or four, etc.).

- One syllable (or two, or three, or four, etc.).

- Short *a* (short *e,* short *i,* etc.).

- Long *a* (long *e,* long *i,* etc.).

- Silent *e.*

- Starts like my name (ends like my name).

- Nouns (verbs, adjectives, etc.).

- Animals (colors, people, numbers, etc.).

You might also include a small table, a desk, or even a low tray (like a tray for serving breakfast in bed) for students to use for writing. This will come in handy for copying words, tracing letters, or other writing tasks that aid in letter and word study. Provide some shelves and/or baskets for storing word study materials. Post alphabet charts that are familiar to your students here, too, as well as word study books (dictionaries, thesauri, word books).

Materials

Materials you might have in the ABC/word study work station include:

- Letter formation cards.

- Magnetic letters.

- Dry-erase board and markers.

- Wikki Stix.

- Play dough.

- Rubber stamp letters.

- ABC posters.

- ABC puzzles.

- ABC books.

- Alphabet tiles.

- Molded tactile letters and tactile letter cards.

- Sponge alphabet letters.

- A Magna Doodle.

- Letter templates.

- Letter-trace cards.

- Link letters.

- Blank books.

- Stickers for making ABC books.

- Paper, pencils, and crayons.

- An interactive word wall.

- A magnetic surface for word sorts and games.

- Magnetic word cards.

- Word cards.

- A pocket chart.

- Word games.

- Dictionaries.

- Thesauri.

- Word books.

A teacher's set of magnetic letters sorted and labeled in a fishing tackle box.

How to Introduce the ABC/Word Study Work Station

The best way to introduce the ABC/word study work station is to begin by teaching with the word wall. If you have student names on the wall at the beginning of the year, show students how to do simple sorts with names. With the whole class, model how to use sorting cards to determine the way the words will be sorted, such as by the number of letters in each name. Teach students to sort and then read the words. You might even have them copy the sort onto a strip of paper for an assessment, if you like.

At the beginning of kindergarten and first grade, you might also provide some ABC puzzles or ABC books. In second grade, add some simple sorting activities with high-frequency words from first grade for review. Or include games they learned in first grade, such as Bingo or Concentration.

Over time, add new activities. Introduce them in a large group first. Many word sorting activities

A black dry-erase board and colored pens add novelty.

Magnetic word cards with words colored according to parts of speech add novelty, too.

can be introduced to the whole group with words printed in large letters on cards. Stamping and tracing letters can be modeled to the whole group. Games like Hangman can be taught to the whole class. Word hunts can be taught to children who already know how to read.

Other activities are better introduced in small groups. Letter sorts might be introduced this way, since you will want to observe students more closely and they will each need their own magnetic letters for sorting. Some word games are also better introduced in small groups, where every child can participate more readily.

What the Teacher Needs to Model

Children sometimes get off-task at the ABC/word study work station. It is important to carefully model the use of materials before placing them in this station. Here are some possibilities for what you might model:

How to sort letters. Use magnetic or foam letters for sorting, since these have a 3-D surface. Students can feel the features of the letters as they manipulate the objects. Begin with an easy task, like sorting letters by color. Tell the children to find all the letters that are red, then all the letters that are blue, and so on. Then move on to sorting by letters with sticks and letters with circles: "Find the letters that have sticks like this. Put all the letters with circles here. Put the letters with dots over here." As children become familiar with these features of letters, teach them the letter names. Some students will need lots of practice with letter sorts, while others will learn their letters very quickly. You might provide cards to help students sort letters. See Appendix F for letter sort cards.

How to correctly form letters. It is important to teach young children correct letter formation as they learn to write letters and words. Emphasize that strokes should go from top to bottom and from left to right. Model letter formation as you write in front of the class. Work with children on letter formation during interactive writing as you share the pen with them. Teach consistent letter formation from one grade level to the next. You might have standard language to use as you teach a letter. For example, "To write *a*, go around, up, and down." Show children how to use letter formation cards for practice.

How to read ABC books. Read some simple alphabet books aloud to young children. Begin with those that have a picture, a letter, and one word per page. Show students how to read and point to the letter and the word. If you use more complex ABC books where children can't read every word, show them how to read the book like a beginning reader. Model how to read the known letter, name the pictures, and say something about the page. For example for *A, My Name Is Alice* by Jane Bayer (1984), a beginning reader might say, "A, my name is Alice and I'm from Alaska. I eat ants. My husband is an anteater. B, my name is Barbara and I sell balloons. I'm a bear."

How to read ABC charts. Read a large ABC chart with the children during shared reading. Demonstrate how to point to each letter, picture, and word as you read together. Use this same chart to help them find letters for spelling words as they write with you. Place small copies of the chart at the work station for children to practice reading. Show them how to read the chart, sing the chart, and match magnetic letters to it.

How to sort words (or pictures). Model sorting with the class using picture cards to start. Show them how to sort by the first sound of each picture. For example, "*Sun, seven,* and *soap* all start the same, *sss,* so we'll put those together. *Moon, man,* and *mouse* start the same, *mmm,* so we'll put those in this row."

Show children how to sort and then read the pictures, checking to be sure the pictures all start with the same sound.

The process is the same for sorting words. Use familiar words that children recognize quickly. Have them sort the words in a variety of ways. (See the suggestions for word sorts given earlier.) Again, have the children sort and read the words. Older students can also record their sorts by copying the words onto paper in separate columns for each. Sheron Brown's *All Sorts of Sorts* (2000) is a great resource for word sorts.

How to do a speed sort. Once students know how to do word sorts, challenge them to do speed sorts. Provide a timer or stopwatch and show them how to use it to record how long it takes to do a particular sort. Encourage them to try to beat their own times. In word sorting, the key is fluency as well as accuracy.

How to go on word hunts. Word hunts provide words for children to sort. Have students look in familiar books that they can already read fluently to find words with a particular feature, such as words that start like *moon,* words that end with *-ed,* or rhyming words. Have them copy each word onto a blank space on a grid. (See Appendix F for a sample word hunt sheet.) After children have filled out their word hunt sheets, have them meet in small groups to cut their words apart and sort their words together. Store words in an envelope with group members' names on it. They can then practice this sort at the ABC/word study work station.

How to play word games. Some word games can be taught to the whole class, such as word wall games like Hangman. Bingo or Wordo (a variation of Bingo using spelling words) can also be taught to the whole group. Other games are better taught in small groups. Games like Memory or Concentration are best played by just a few children at a time. Use the many commercially produced word games in

Two children play Hangman with word wall words.

small groups, too. Teach the game first and then place it in the work station.

How to use and store ABC materials. Be sure that everything in the ABC/word study work station has a container with a label on it so materials can easily be put away. You might have the students help you make the labels to promote ownership at this work station. For younger students, use pictures on the labels. Old school supply catalogs are a great source of pictures for labels.

If you're using magnetic letters at this station, you might not want to put out a whole tackle box filled with letters. This may be too much for young children to manage. Instead, you might place letters needed in zip-lock bags, or put out a partially filled box.

How to use dictionaries and word books. Model the use of the dictionary as you read aloud to students and come across interesting or unusual words. Show students how to look up a word's meaning or pronunciation. Also model how to use the dictionary to check the spelling of words. As you write with children, show them how to use a thesaurus. The more you use these resources yourself, the more likely your students will be to use them. Provide a variety of dictionaries and beginning thesauri. Include picture dictionaries in English as well as other languages.

You might also have word play books available. *My First Word Board Book* by Angela Wilkes (1997) is a sturdy little board book that young children will love to explore. Use this book (and others in the series) in a modeled writing lesson to show how one gets ideas for writing and how to use the book to spell words. Students might like making their own pages for a similar book. They could, for example, make a word book about animals or one about plants.

Magnetic letters matched to alphabet attached to a magnetic surface.

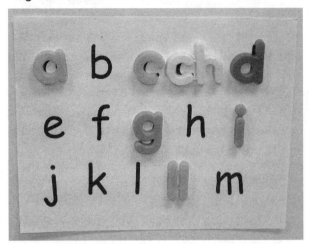

ABC/Word Study Work Station Possibilities

Here are some ideas for the ABC/word study work station for kindergarten, first grade, and second grade.

Kindergarten

Purposes:

- Learn visual features of letters to assist in letter identification.

- Identify letters automatically.

Materials:

- Magnetic letters.

- Letter sorting cards.

- Play dough.

- Alphabet feature Bingo game.

Possible "I Can" list (brainstorm ideas with students):

I can . . .

- Use letter sorting cards.

- Make letters with play dough.

- Play Alphabet Bingo.

Assessment and evaluation ideas:

- Observe letter sorting.

- Are students increasing their understanding of how letters are made? Can they identify which letters have sticks or circles or both?

- Watch children as they play Alphabet Bingo. Are they locating letters with certain visual features (dots, circles, slants, etc.) more and more quickly?

- Are students improving their performance of letter identification tasks? Can they name more letters?

- Can they find matching letters with a variety of fonts?

First Grade

Purpose:

- Recognize and spell high-frequency words correctly.

Materials:

- Word wall words.

- A magnetic area for sorting.

- Magnetic letters.

- A dry-erase board and markers.

- Letter stamps and stamp pad.

- Blank paper.

- Paper for recording word sorts.

- Pencils.

Possible "I Can" list (brainstorm ideas with students):

I can . . .

- Stamp and read word wall words.

- Make and read word wall words with magnetic letters.

- Sort words and record my sort on list paper.

- Find, read, and write word wall words from my books.

Assessment and evaluation ideas:

- Collect and look at students' stamped words. Are words spelled correctly? Can they read the words? Are they using the words correctly in their daily writing?

- Are the children sorting and reading words correctly? Look at their recorded word lists as well as their physical word sorts.

- Are the children increasing their instant recognition of these words as they read?

Second Grade

Purposes:

- Write with more proficient spelling of inflectional endings, including plurals and verb tenses.

- Learn to use a dictionary to build word meanings and to confirm pronunciation of words.

Materials:

- Word wall words.

- Word hunt sheets.

- Scissors, pencils, and envelopes (for cutting apart word hunt sheets and storing word cards).

- Familiar books for word hunts.

- Early dictionaries (appropriate for second graders).

- A word study (spiral) notebook for each child.

Possible "I Can" list (brainstorm ideas with students):

I can . . .

- Sort word wall words with endings.

- Hunt for words that end in *-s, -es,* and *-ies* in my books.

- Hunt for words that end in *-ed* or *-ing* in my books.

- Write words I find on my word hunt sheets.

- Sort words on my word hunt sheets.

- Record my sorts on list paper and write what I learned from doing this sort.

- Use the dictionary to look up words from my reading and/or writing.

- Record what I found out in the dictionary in my word study notebook.

Assessment and evaluation ideas:

- Collect students' recorded sorts and read about what they learned. Are they able to articulate the principles they are learning?

■ Observe the children's sorting. Are they sorting correctly? Are they reading their sorts with accuracy? Are they sorting more quickly?

■ Look at students' writing. Are they spelling more words that end in -s, -es,- ies, -ed, and -ing correctly?

■ Do students use any of their new words from dictionary work in their speaking or writing? Encourage them to do so.

■ Do you notice children using the dictionary more frequently and with greater ease? Are they paying attention to new words and discussing them in class?

How to Solve Problems That May Arise

Because so many materials are suitable for the ABC/word study work station, it may be tempting to put out many materials too quickly. Teach with the materials first, and put them in the station gradually. Don't put out too much or the children will have trouble keeping the area neat. It is better to remove materials students are losing interest in and replace these with something new and fresh than simply to keep adding more and more materials.

Of course, the opposite of this problem is to not have enough for children to do. Don't put out just one task a week for students to complete. If you do that, some children will finish before everyone else and may become bored. The key to success at this work station is to provide a variety of interesting activities that you've already introduced so students know how to use them.

As mentioned previously, you might also provide labels to help children know where to return each item after it is used. When this work station gets disorganized, problems often begin. For example, children will become frustrated doing a puzzle

with missing pieces. It is difficult to play a game when all the pieces are not in the correct box. You might consider having a box labeled "Missing Pieces" in this work station, into which students can place incomplete games and leftover pieces. Have a materials manager check this work station daily to be sure everything is in working order.

Differentiating at This Work Station

The ABC/word study work station is one at which differentiation is crucial. At the beginning of the year, you will probably introduce a variety of tasks to students. However, over time you must start to differentiate them to make this station meaningful to the students working there. Observe students to see which need practice with letter identification tasks and which are ready to make sentences with word cards. Then assign specific tasks to groups of students based on need. An easy way to do this is to provide color-coded shelves or baskets for different levels of materials. Or you can place colored dots on materials to match the word study level. For example, letter identification tasks might be in green baskets or have green dots on them. Tell children who need this kind of practice to choose from the green activities. Or post a chart in the station with colored squares and students' names written on clothespins and clipped to the appropriate color on the chart as an indication of what they might work on.

Another possibility is to use word study task cards. Linda Dorn has created sets of these, available from the Teaching Resource Center at www.trcabc .com. She describes their use in her book *Shaping Literate Minds* (2002). Another good resource for word study activities is *Words Their Way* by Donald Bear et al. (2000). This book describes various spelling stages and appropriate activities for each stage. Many games for word study follow-up and practice can be taught and then used indepen-

Color-coded shelves and tubs with matching colored dots provide activities for four different groups.

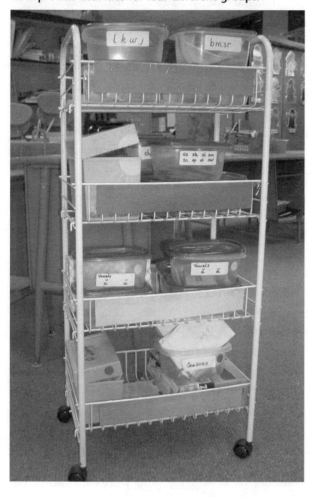

You might want to make a folder to keep track of where students are in their word study. Open a manila folder and draw a horizontal and a vertical line to create four quadrants. Each will represent a word study level of students in your classroom. (If your students are at more than four different levels, make two folders with four levels written on each.) Take the list of activities above and write one at the top of each quadrant. Then write each child's name on a small sticky note and place it in the appropriate space. This will enable you easily to keep track of who needs to go to which level of activity. If you like, color code the spaces by coloring each space to match the levels above. As students move through different levels of word study, simply move their name to the appropriate space.

If you use the word study levels in Bear's *Words Their Way,* use those spelling stages (emergent, letter name–alphabetic, within-word pattern, syllables and affixes, derivational relations) for your labels. Decide on a color to represent each stage and color-code the activities accordingly. In addition, if you meet with word study groups, students can practice their word study activities more frequently: they can do them during word study time as well as when they visit the ABC/word study work station.

dently at this work station. Again, games may be placed in colored folders or color-coded zip-lock bags to differentiate levels. For example, here is a hierarchy of some levels to consider along with a possible color-coding system:

1. Letter identification—green.
2. Beginning sound work—yellow.
3. Ending sound work—blue.
4. Blends and digraphs—red.
5. Short vowel work—orange.
6. Long vowel work—purple.
7. Syllable work—pink.
8. Prefixes and suffixes—brown.

A word study folder made from a manila folder to show which students need which materials for letter/word study.

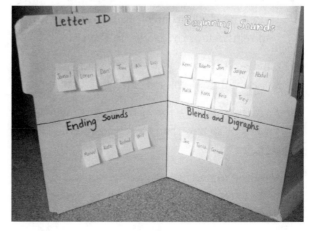

Ways to Keep This Station Going Throughout the Year

To make this station effective all year, be careful to keep it uncluttered. It is easy to continuously add new material as you teach. But soon you'll run out of space. Be sure to remove some things that children have mastered. For example, if, by October, most of your first graders can identify alphabet letters, put away the letter games and have students make known words with magnetic letters instead. Here are some ideas to help you add interest to the station throughout the year:

- Change the words on the wall throughout the year. At the beginning of the year, start with children's names. Add high-frequency words that the children need to know how to read and write at their grade level. As you notice students spelling the words correctly in their writing, make a ceremony of removing those words from the wall. Add new words that represent spelling patterns your students are learning, too. In mid-first and in second grade, you might add homophones on different colored cards. For example, put *to* on a blue card, *two* on yellow, and *too* on pink. Then refer to that spelling by color ("Use the yellow *two* if you're spelling the number word").

- Add new word study games over time. Remove those that students aren't using as frequently and reintroduce them later in the year.

- Change the words in the word study games. Or use different-colored cards in a new game.

- Vary the materials for writing. Use crayons for a week or so and then switch to colored chalk or paint.

- Vary the materials for making words. Use magnetic letters until interest in these wanes. Then move on to Wikki Stix or play dough for nov-

elty. Ask for the students' input on which materials they'd like to change.

- Replace the small dry-erase boards with small chalkboards. Or substitute a black dry-erase board for a white one. Office supply stores sell black marker boards and special colored pens for writing on them.

- Add new word study books. Invite students to make their own or bring some from home to add to your collection.

- Let older students design their own task cards for things to do at this station.

How to Assess/Keep Kids Accountable

How will you know if students are actually getting something out of this station? This is the question teachers ask most frequently about work stations generally, but especially about the ABC/word study work station. To answer this question, you must begin by assessing your students *before* you send them to this station. First, look at your students' writing to determine where they are in their understanding of how letters and words function. Ask yourself, as Donald Bear does, "What is the child *using but confusing*?" Bear notes that spelling is a window into the child's understanding of print. Also look at running records you have taken of the student's oral reading. Look for patterns of sounds the child is "using but confusing."

Once you know what a child is using but confusing, you can assign activities for that specific skill. (Use the color-coding system mentioned earlier for ideas on how to let each child know what to practice. The folder in which you record the word study level of each child will come in handy here.) For example, if a child is writing mock letters, he is *using* letter-like forms but is *confusing* what letters are. That child will benefit from letter identification work, such as letter sorts. Likewise, if a student is misspelling long vowel patterns but is writing short vowel sounds correctly, that child is *using but confusing* long vowels. She should do word hunts and sorts with a particular long vowel pattern, such as long *a*. She might also play word games that focus on long *a* words. (See Chapter 10 for further ideas on using assessment to decide which tasks are best suited for different children.)

Finally, assess how each child is doing after a few rounds of practice. There are several ways to do this second assessment. One way is to look at the students' writing again after they have practiced for a while. Do you see a change in their spelling and/or writing? Another way to assess is to listen to them read and see if they are more easily decoding words with whatever pattern they were having trouble with. You should see a direct correlation. If you don't, go back and reteach the pattern in a small-group setting. Also, plan to observe students at the ABC/word study work station. Are they using the materials assigned? Are they practicing in the way you demonstrated?

Helping students find activities that are on their level will help them get more from this work station. Children who are practicing tasks that are at their instructional level will generally stay more focused because they can be successful at them. There should be just a bit of challenge or problem solving involved in a task to engage the learner.

Here are a few other ways to keep students accountable at the ABC/word study work station:

- Where appropriate, provide paper for students to record the sorts they are doing. Also have them write about what they learned by doing the sort. Check to see if their understanding of the word pattern is increasing.

- Use the form in Appendix F to observe students at this station. Once a week, take a few minutes to walk around the classroom and jot down notes about what you notice students doing at this station. Share the good things you are noticing with the class.

- Periodically, have students share what they have learned at the ABC/word study work station during work station sharing time. Have them show something they made or tell about what they learned while they were practicing there. For example, a child in kindergarten might show the class his favorite ABC book and read a page or two. A first grader might show a word hunt sheet for short vowels, and a second-grade student might tell about all the different spellings she found for the long *e* sound (*ee*, *ea*, *e*-consonant-*e*, just *e*).

Reflection and Dialogue

Consider the following:

1. Where have you placed your ABC/word study work station? Can children easily use the word wall words? How have you made your word wall interactive? If you're having trouble with placement of your word wall or making it interactive, consult a colleague or two for help.

2. How have you organized the ABC/word study work station? Can students easily find the materials they need? Are they returning materials to the proper place? Take a "field trip" to a colleague's classroom to see his or her ABC/word study work station. Share your ideas and observations with each other.

3. Are students interrupting you when they are at the work station? If so, what is the nature of the interruption? Were they arguing? Did they need help with directions? Were materials missing? Reread the section on How to Solve Problems and make changes to this station as needed. Reteach expectations in mini-lessons if necessary.

4. Observe students to see if they are doing the activities you assigned to them. Use the form in Appendix F as you "eyeball" this station several times during literacy work station time. Try to watch those students who need the most practice to see if they are doing what they should.

5. Do you have a variety of activities for students to choose from at this station? How have you differentiated them? Share your ideas with a colleague.

6. What new word study activities can you introduce to the group as a whole? In a small-group setting?

7. How are you keeping records of your students' understanding of letters and words? Do you have a folder or checklist to keep track of phonemic awareness levels, letter identification, and/or spelling patterns that students have mastered? Share your system with a colleague.

8. Are you bogged down in paperwork generated from this station? If so, determine which types of written work best demonstrate what students are learning here. Get rid of extraneous written tasks you may have instituted here in the name of "accountability."

8

Poetry Work Station

It's spring in this kindergarten classroom. The room is filled with paintings of flowers, blue skies, and butterflies. In the poetry work station, several charts with poems copied onto them are clipped on individual skirt hangers, which hang from a metal drying rack, so children can easily slide the hangers over to read the next poem.

> I'm glad the sky is painted blue,
> And the earth is painted green,
> With such a lot of nice fresh air
> All sandwiched in between.

Simon and Lindsay chant this poem together as they point to the words printed in black ink on a large chart. It is a poem they know well. Their teacher has read it with them many times during shared reading. It's perfect for them because it's short and has many words they know, including some color words. When they're finished reading, they play a little game they call "I Know a Word" with small, precut pieces of highlighter tape that are just the right size for covering a word. Simon goes first. "I know *and,*" he says and covers it with highlighter tape. Lindsay goes next. "I know *blue*. It's a color word and is on our color chart over there," she states proudly. The children take turns covering up words until they have identified almost all of them.

Then they turn their attention to a new activity. Lindsay says, "You know how the teacher showed us how to write poems? I'm going to write a color poem. 'Blue, blue. Blue like the pool.'"

"I'm going to write one, too," chimes in Simon. "Mine's going to be about my dog. 'My big dog Luke has lots of spots.'" The children write their poems using their own spelling onto paper stored in this station. After work station time today, they'll read their poems with the rest of the class during sharing time. Then their teacher will copy their poems (using conventional spelling) onto large charts for the children to read with their friends. The class will read them during shared reading, too.

In a first-grade room down the hall, two children meet in the poetry station and read poems together, too. Their poems are more challenging and a bit longer than those read by the kindergartners. But sometimes the first graders still like to play I Know a Word, which they learned the previous year. They also enjoy taking photocopies of poems they love from a tub in the poetry station, reading and illustrating them, and adding these to their poetry notebooks, half-inch three-ring binders into which they place favorite poems. Each time children read a poem out of their notebook to someone, they put a mark at the bottom of the page to keep track of how often they've read it. This encourages lots of practice and promotes fluent reading, too.

In a second-grade classroom in the same building, another group of children is in their poetry station. They are browsing through tubs of poetry books. They are familiar with many of the poets because they have studied some of them in class. "Listen to this one by David McCord," Sondra says to Will. "I love this 'every time I climb a tree' part." She reads the poem aloud to him. "I'm thinking about learning it by memory but it's kind of long.

Which one are you going to memorize?" One of the tasks at this work station is to learn a poem and dramatize it for the class.

What the Children Do

The poetry work station is a natural place for children to play with words and enjoy language. Throughout the year, many of the activities will remain the same. What changes is the level and sophistication of the poems. As children grow as readers, the poems placed in this station become more challenging. New poems are introduced regularly through shared reading, so there is always something new at this station. Here are some possibilities of what students might do at the poetry work station. As children try each activity, it may be posted on the "I Can" chart:

■ *Reading a poem.* Poems may be handwritten or typed onto a chart, sentence strips, or a card. Poems written by the class and by individual students can be put into books and placed in a tub labeled "Poetry Books."

■ *Buddy reading a poem.* Children read familiar poems with partners. Matching poems may be

After reading a poem to a friend, a child adds another mark to the bottom of the page of her poetry notebook.

Buddy reading a poem written on matching cards.

Illustrating a poem.

Two students work together to sequence the lines of a poem.

glued to pairs of cards with matching colors to help students find the same poem.

■ *Illustrating a poem.* Provide a basket with photocopied poems in it. Children can take any poem from the container and illustrate it. The poems can later be placed in the child's poetry notebook or in a box labeled "Finished Work" for the teacher to grade.

■ *Filling in the blanks.* Copy a poem onto chart paper and leave blanks for some of the letters. For example, *Rain on the green gr____.* Laminate the chart. Then tell children to have the poem make sense by filling in the missing part(s) with a marker. Include a smaller version of the complete poem for self-checking.

■ *Building a poem.* Write a poem line by line on sentence strips for children to reassemble, in sequence, in a pocket chart. Again provide a small copy of the poem for self-checking.

■ *Changing a poem.* Provide sticky notes so students can substitute other words in a poem

and play with language. If some lines are cut into individual words, children can also experiment with changing the word order. When they are finished, have them copy their "new poem" and share it with the class.

■ *Copying a poem.* For handwriting practice, have children choose favorite poems from poetry books at the work station and copy them into the child's personal poetry notebook.

Changing a poem by replacing old words with new ones written on sticky notes.

Students copy poems into their poetry notebooks for handwriting practice.

Two children enjoy listening to a poem together and following along in a book.

A student tapes her reading of a poem to take home and listen to in the car.

■ *Listening to a poem.* Let children listen to favorite poems by adding a tape recorder to the poetry work station. You can use commercial tapes or make your own.

■ *Tape recording a poem and taking it home to listen to in the car.* Teach children how to make their own tape recording. They can then listen to their own reading and assess their own fluency. They can also listen to the tape in their car and memorize some poems that way.

■ *Writing a poem.* Teach children how to write their own poems and let them compose the poems either at this station or at the writing work station.

■ *Making a poem with magnetic words.* Provide either a commercially produced magnetic poetry kit or make your own with your computer and magnetic paper, available where office supplies are sold.

■ *Finding special words or kinds of words in a poem.* Students can use highlighter tape to mark rhyming words or words that have a certain sound. Provide paper for them to record the words they found, if you like.

Children find words with the *ou* sound and mark them with highlighter tape.

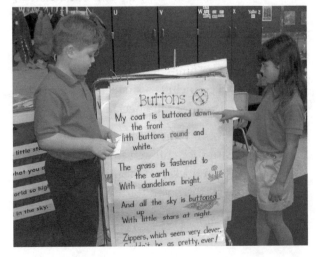

■ *Finding a pattern in the poem.* Have children name and chart the pattern for a particular rhyming poem. "One, Two, Buckle My Shoe" is a poem that follows the pattern AA, BB, CC, DD, EE.

■ *Comparing two poems.* Show children how to use a Venn diagram to compare ideas in two poems. It's easiest if you start with paired poems about the same topic. (See the example in Figure 8.1.) For this, use a pocket folder turned inside out, with a poem glued to each side of the folder and a Venn diagram sheet in a pocket at the back.

■ *Memorizing and performing a poem.* Challenge students to memorize a poem of their choice once every six to nine weeks. Let them practice at the poetry work station and perform the poem for a friend. Simple props can be made available for dramatization.

■ *Reading about poets.* Create an author study about a poet. Include information about the author as well as sample poems by that poet. (See Figure 8.2.) Appendix G provides a suggested list of poets to study by grade level, as well as a list of recommended books of poems.

How to Set Up the Poetry Work Station

You don't need a very large space for a poetry work station. You might hang charts from a stand or rack of some sort. Positioning the stand at a ninety-degree angle from the wall can create an inviting nook for reading and writing poetry. (Just be sure it's not blocking your view.) Or use a science project board and copy poems onto large legal-sized paper posted there to create a space for reading and writing poetry.

Figure 8.1 Paired Poems

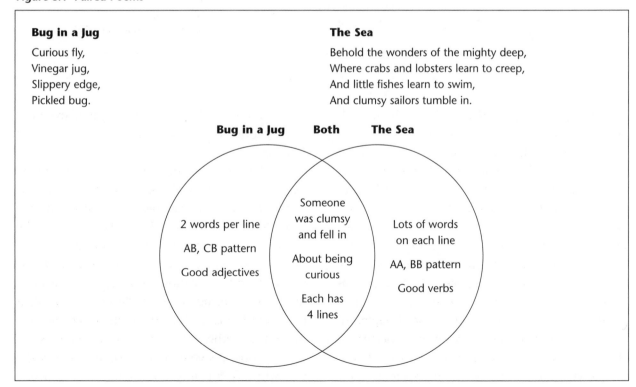

Bug in a Jug

Curious fly,
Vinegar jug,
Slippery edge,
Pickled bug.

The Sea

Behold the wonders of the mighty deep,
Where crabs and lobsters learn to creep,
And little fishes learn to swim,
And clumsy sailors tumble in.

Bug in a Jug   Both   The Sea

2 words per line

AB, CB pattern

Good adjectives

Someone was clumsy and fell in

About being curious

Each has 4 lines

Lots of words on each line

AA, BB pattern

Good verbs

Figure 8.2 Author Study for Poetry

Peter Fox Photography

Poet: Betsy Franco

Betsy Franco has three boys. They have given her many of her ideas for writing. One of her sons, James, co-starred in the movie *Spider-Man*!

Betsy has written more than 40 poetry books! She also likes to put together anthologies of other poets' writing. She writes all kinds of books, from poetry to nonfiction.

Betsy studied art in college. But she decided to become a writer. She thinks that part of being a writer is being stubborn and not giving up on your ideas.

Betsy and her husband live in California.

Here are some of Betsy's poems:

Camping

Picking up branches,
Lighting the matches.
Sitting on boxes,
Seeing some foxes.
Cooking the dinner,
Washing the dishes.
Watching the moon,
Sharing our wishes.

Swinging

I jump on the swing,
You give me a push.
I pump and I pump,
The air goes whoosh.

I pump and I pump,
I'm up past the park.
I'm up past the clouds,
I swing till it's dark.

Cool Rocks

Flat rocks,
Round rocks,
Skip-them-on-the-pond rocks.
Rough rocks,
Neat rocks,
Kick-them-down-the-street rocks.
Rare rocks,
Grand rocks,
Hold-them-in-your-hand rocks!

Include poems written on large charts with thick black marker. You might hang each chart from a skirt hanger with clips, as mentioned earlier. Or use a metal coat hanger with the chart stapled over and around it. You can also use commercially produced poetry charts. There are many fine ones with beautiful illustrations. Some companies even make accompanying sentence strips with the poems printed on them line by line. If you choose to use these, you might include a pocket chart in this station as well. Or you might prefer to place them in a separate pocket chart work station (see Chapter 9). Some teachers also put an overhead projector on the floor or on a low cart at the poetry work station and have poems available on transparencies for children to read. Others set up a separate overhead work station with additional activities (again, see Chapter 9).

In kindergarten and early first grade, many teachers put some of the same poems in multiple work stations. For example, they might include "Row, Row, Row Your Boat" on a large chart in the poetry work station, on a transparency at the overhead work station, and on sentence strips at the pocket chart work station. This encourages flexibility of text, or recognition that "Row, row, row your boat" says the same thing no matter where one sees it—on the overhead, on a chart, on a sentence strip, or in a book. It's your choice. You might start the year with just a poetry work station and gradually

Poems are hung from metal clothes hangers for easy access.

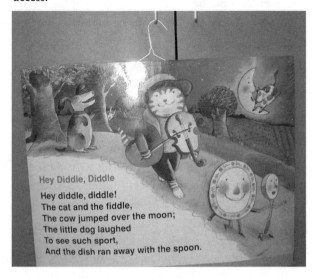

Use clear packing tape to secure the hanger to the back of each poetry chart.

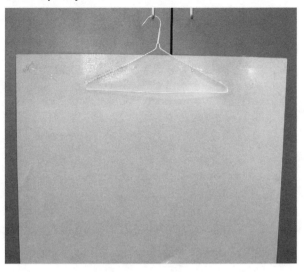

add an overhead and a pocket chart. Or you might choose to set these up as two completely separate work stations.

You'll also want to put at least one tub of poetry books in this work station. Begin with just one or two books. As you read poems from additional poetry books for children, add these to the tubs. Children will return to their favorites to read and reread, if you have modeled this. Also include a container with multiple copies of favorite poems. Children can use these for buddy reading. Again, be sure the poems are familiar to the students so they can be successful with them on their own. And be sure to include some student-written poems on charts. You might also make a book entitled "Our Poems" and place it in the tub of poetry books.

Over time, add a container with photocopied poems for the children. Be sure the print is large enough for students to read easily. They can read and illustrate the sheets and add them to their poetry notebooks.

If you want something different at this station, you might convert it to a songs work station at some point in the year. Young children love to sing songs and will often learn them quickly. You might copy some of their favorite songs onto charts. If you

teach kindergarten, don't put too much print on the chart because it may be hard for students to follow along. You might just copy a favorite stanza or verse. Read aloud picture books that are also songs and add a tub labeled "Songs Books" to this station. Even young children can begin to distinguish the differences between songs and poems and learn how they recite poems but sing songs. You might ask the music teacher for words to songs students are learning in music class and include some of these in the work station, too.

Changing the poetry work station to a songs work station adds novelty.

Materials

Start simply. Begin with poems used in shared reading. Over the course of the year, include some of the following at the poetry work station:

- Tub(s) of favorite poetry books, perhaps sorted by poets.

- Poems copied onto large chart paper.

- Smaller copies of poems mounted on tagboard and laminated (for buddy reading).

- Jump-rope rhymes and tongue twisters.

- A tub of songbooks.

- Paired poems (see Figure 8.1).

- A magnetic poetry kit (available commercially, or can be teacher-made).

- Poet study information (see Figure 8.2).

- Pointers in a container.

- Wikki Stix.

- Highlighter tape, precut and stuck to an index card.

- Photocopied poems in a container.

- Paper (for copying favorite poems or writing your own).

- Pencils and crayons.

- Magazine pictures (for inspiring children's poems).

- Photos of your students in action—on field trips, in performances, etc. (for inspiring children's poems).

- Copies of student-written poems (both in chart form and photocopies).

- A children's rhyming dictionary.

- Sticky notes and a thesaurus (for changing words in poems).

- Simple props (for dramatizing poems).

How to Introduce the Poetry Work Station

Introduce the poetry station during shared reading. As you read favorite and new poems with children, model the reading strategies you'd like them to practice when they go to the poetry work station. Start with a simple task, such as simply reading the poems so they sound like talking. On the "I Can" board, add a card that says "Read poems so it sounds like talking." You might add a second card that says "Point and read." Over time, as you slowly introduce new tasks, add new cards to the "I Can" chart. Also add new poems over time to keep interest at this station.

What the Teacher Needs to Model

The poetry work station will be most successful if you model the following routines over time. Many models, not just one, are needed for children to do their best. Model first; then repeat the activity with children, either in large or small groups, to be sure they understand before moving the activity to the work station.

How to read a poem fluently. In shared reading show children how to read across to the end of a line in a smooth voice, pausing only at the end. Run your finger under the words in a phrased way. Try echo reading, where you read a line and then have children be your echo to give them a feel for fluent reading. Encourage them to "read it so it sounds like talking."

How to read with good expression. Remind children to use an interesting voice to make the poem sound appealing to an audience. Again, try echo reading. Model, then ask students to repeat you. Find poems with lots of feeling or words printed in bold and/or italic type and show children how to add more vibrancy to the reading.

How to find rhyming words. During shared reading, play around with rhyming words. Teach children to listen for words that sound the same at the end (not at the beginning, which is what they are often used to listening for). Use tools, such as highlighter tape and Wikki Stix, to have children mark rhyming words. Also model for them how to make rhyming words with magnetic letters, often by changing just the first letter or two. Show them how to record the rhyming words on list paper.

How to determine the pattern of the poem. Connect literacy to math by helping children think about the pattern of a poem. Tell them that "Twinkle, Twinkle Little Star" is AA, BB, because the first two lines rhyme and so do the last two. You might use Unifix cubes to show the pattern. Encourage students to identify the patterns of new poems you introduce. You might even list the names of poems that have the same patterns.

How to make connections. Model how to write what a poem reminds you of during shared reading. Write your personal connection on a large sticky note and initial it. Place it on the poetry chart beside the line that reminded you of the connection. Then invite students to do the same. This way they can read both the poem and the connections, as well as add their own.

How to create visual images. As you read a poem aloud, stop and explain to students what you see in your mind. Be specific; include colors, sizes, and so on. For example, you might say, "As I read 'Humpty Dumpty had a great fall,' I see this big

Students write their connections on sticky notes and add them to a poetry chart.

white egg falling from a tall wall. The egg looks scared and his arms wave in the air while he's falling." You might even draw a picture and think aloud about your visual image as you do so. Invite students to share their visual images from the poem with each other, as well as with you. They might draw pictures, too.

How to illustrate a poem. Provide art materials that students may use to illustrate poems. Show them how to use these materials so there won't be any problems. For example, if you include watercolors, model and explain how to mix them with water and how to clean up.

How to buddy read a poem. Show children how to read in sync with a partner. You might have them

Children write their own poems using student models posted nearby.

read from one large chart or have double copies of poems in a "buddy poems" basket.

How to write a poem. Adding poems written by children is a good way to keep interest high at this station. Since many teachers don't feel comfortable composing poetry in front of their students, Regie Routman suggests that you teach children how to write poems with kids' poems. Her book, *Kids' Poems* (2000), includes poems written by children and teaching ideas geared to your specific grade level. She takes you step by step through the process of how to teach children what poems are and how to write them. She suggests that poetry is a wonderful form of writing for young children because it requires such a small number of words. You can show children how to take something they've seen or felt and write about it in just a few words in a poem. Emphasize that poems don't have to rhyme.

How to compare two poems. Use paired poems such as those provided in Appendix G. Read the poems with the class and create a Venn diagram that compares and contrasts the two. Show students how to think about meaning, structure (rhyming patterns, alliteration, number of lines, etc.), and kinds of words used (good verbs, lots of adjectives, etc.).

Students use a Venn diagram to compare two poems.

Poetry Work Station Possibilities

Here are some ideas for the poetry work station for different levels.

Kindergarten–Early First Grade

Purposes:

- Become aware of print by one-to-one matching.

- Listen for rhyming words.

- Find high-frequency words.

Materials:

- Familiar poems.

- Pointers.

- Highlighter tape.

Possible "I Can" list (brainstorm ideas with students):

Sample "I Can" list for the poetry work station.

I can . . .

- Read so it sounds like talking.
- Point and read.
- Find rhyming words.
- Find words I know.

Assessment and evaluation ideas:

- Observe one-to-one matching.

- Listen to students read their highlighted words (rhyming/high frequency) and note their accuracy.

- Listen to students read a favorite poetry chart aloud during work station sharing time and note their fluency and expression.

Mid-to-Late First Grade– Second Grade

Purposes:

- Create mental images to improve comprehension.

- Use neat handwriting to make writing easier for others to read.

- Read fluently and with good expression.

Materials:

- Pens, pencils, and crayons.

- Paper.

- Tubs of poetry books.

- Photocopies of poems.

Possible "I Can" list (brainstorm ideas with students):

I can . . .

- Read poems by myself so it sounds like talking.

- Read poems with good expression.

- Read poems fluently with a buddy.

- Copy a favorite poem with neat handwriting so I can easily reread it.

- Put my favorite poem in my poetry notebook and reread it.

- Read a poem, think about the mental image it creates, then draw a picture of that image.

- Share my mental image with a buddy who read the same poem and compare our images.

Assessment and evaluation ideas:

- Look at children's poetry notebooks and take a handwriting grade. Is their handwriting becoming more legible?

- Listen to children read their poems and take a fluency grade. Is fluency improving?

- Have students tape-record their reading of several poems and listen to this. They might do a self-assessment of their fluency. You can also use the tape to assess students' fluency.

How to Solve Problems That May Arise

The biggest problem at the poetry work station is usually boredom. Novelty will help this work station stay interesting. Ask children for ideas of what they'd like to do. Their ideas may give you a fresh perspective. If children tire of this station, you might change it into a songwriting station for a change of pace. (See the suggestions given earlier in this chapter.) The addition of music and possibly even rhythm instruments can make the old poems new again. Include patriotic songs in this station, too. Another idea is to highlight tongue twisters for a few weeks or turn the poetry station into a jump-rope-rhyme station temporarily, complete with jump-rope rhymes on tape for them to chant along with. (You can make the tape yourself, or get some of your fluent readers to make it for you.)

Another problem I've seen for some emergent readers is that the poems in the station are too hard for them to read. If you notice children playing around in this station and not being on task, you might ask them to read some of the poems for you. I did this recently in a kindergarten and found that the two girls there couldn't read any of the poems in the station! Even though the teacher had "taught" the poems earlier in the year, the selections had too many lines and too many unfamiliar

words for these emergent readers. Choose poems for emergent students with just four to six lines of text and words they know at the beginning of each line for them to use as "anchors." A wonderful resource for this is Betsy Franco's *My Very Own Poetry Collection: 101 Poems for Kindergartners* (2002).

Differentiating at This Work Station

Be sure to provide poems at a variety of levels for your students at the poetry station. You might put colored dots on some of them for the various levels—for example, easier poems might have green dots, and harder poems, purple dots. Let children buddy read at this station to provide support for those who need it. Include some poems for two voices as well. The more you teach with poems in shared reading, the more successful your students will be at the poetry station if you place those poems here after you work with them.

Ways to Keep This Station Going Throughout the Year

Adding new touches on a regular basis will keep the poetry work station alive. Remember to add only one new item at a time to keep things novel. Here are some ideas for keeping this station interesting:

- Change the poems as often as needed. Read them together repeatedly in shared reading first.

- Add new poetry books, especially those you've read aloud.

- Add a new poet study tub. Begin to study the poet together first.

- Add a new kind of paper for copying poems for a poetry notebook.

- Provide shape paper for copying poems for the poetry notebook.

- Add a new medium for illustrating poems, such as craypas or watercolors. Model how to use these first.

- Add a three-ring notebook labeled "Our Favorite Poems" and let children copy and illustrate favorites and place them in the notebook for others to read.

- Write poems with your class and add these poems to this station.

- Change the station to one focusing on songwriting or tongue twisters or jump-rope rhymes.

- Add digital photos of your class to provide inspiration for students writing their own poems.

- Add soft rhythm instruments and model how to use these (quietly).

- Highlight a child's "Poetry Picks of the Week" on a poster in the poetry station. Feature a different child each week. Save the old posters and hang them up for children to peruse.

- Add magazine pictures to help spark ideas for writing poems.

- Add a rhyming dictionary and model how to use it. Scholastic's *Rhyming Dictionary* is a great resource.

How to Assess/Keep Kids Accountable

Ask students to share their favorite poems with the class after work station time. You might also have children memorize and perform poems. A sense of audience will contribute greatly to accountability at this station. Also collect students' poetry notebooks (if they have them) and review them for assessment.

If you have children look for certain kinds of words at this work station, you can periodically have them write the words they found on list paper and use these lists in grading. Another way to gauge how students are doing at this station is to use the form in Appendix G. Observe several students at a time and look for reading strategies appropriate for their reading levels. For example, with emergent readers watch for one-to-one matching and return sweep. With early readers, listen for reading fluency. With more fluent readers, watch for phrased, expressive reading.

Reflection and Dialogue

Consider the following:

1. Observe several groups of children in your poetry work station. What do they spend most of their time doing? Which activities do they enjoy most? Least? Talk with them about what they are learning in this station. Share your findings with a colleague.

2. Do you enjoy reading poetry? Teaching with poetry? Writing poetry? How is this reflected in what you see happening at the poetry work station?

3. What kinds of poems do your students seem to like best? Who are their favorite poets? Find more poems related to their interests to build enthusiasm for this station. Ask your colleagues to be on the lookout for poems for you.

4. Have a poetry hunting party with your team. Bring your favorite poetry resources and ask them to do the same. Hunt for poems with lots of high-frequency words that your children need for reading and writing. Share with each other.

5. Build a poetry resource notebook of your own. Divide it into sections labeled by topic, such as animals, holidays, sports, plants, back to school, and so forth. Keep copies of favorite poems in here for easy access.

9

Other Work Stations

Chapters 3 through 8 explained in detail how to set up six basic literacy work stations in your classroom. However, there are many more possibilities for other stations. This chapter outlines a variety of additional stations and includes ideas on how to add literacy to traditional kindergarten centers. Use the same principles outlined in the previous chapters to help you set up these work stations.

You might begin with the literacy work stations described in the previous chapters and then gradually introduce other stations throughout the school year. Or you might substitute one of the stations described in this chapter, if the materials are more readily available or if the station seems easier for you to implement. The stations suggested here are options for you to consider as you expand this approach to meaningful independent work in your classroom. Choose what works for you.

Computer Work Station

In a kindergarten classroom with only one computer, two students sit at it and share the tasks. One child uses the mouse, and the other controls the keyboard. Their teacher has downloaded several games they can play and has bookmarked them. The children begin by playing a spelling game that the teacher has demonstrated. When they have finished playing, they switch roles: the child with the mouse changes places with the one who had the keyboard. This time they read along with a story on an interactive CD. One child puts the CD in the computer and the other will put it away when they have finished. The children enjoy their early success with using a computer.

In a second-grade classroom in another district there is a bank of computers. Four students come to this station at a time to use the four computers. Each child works at his or her own tasks. One stu-

A Kid Pix story written and illustrated on the computer.

Computer games already taught are posted on the "I Can" list.

dent is using Kid Pix to add pictures to a story written on a previous day. Another is typing a new story. The other two students are creating simple Power Point presentations on books read during independent reading. At this school, the students have learned how to use Kid Pix and Power Point in the computer lab. Their teacher has many choices for expanding literacy through computers because her district has a large technology budget. Many of her students have computers at home and practice there as well.

Ideas for the Work Station

Even if you have only one computer in your classroom, you can have a computer work station. The most important thing to remember at this station, as at others, is that modeling must take place to enable students to use the materials here effectively. Children should not be sitting at the computer playing the same game over and over or drawing pictures for the entire time. There are many worthwhile programs students can use at this station; just remember to add options, one at a time, throughout the school year. Here are some possibilities for what might be included on the "I Can" list at this station:

I can . . .

- Play a game.

- Listen to a book on a CD.

- Read along with a book on a CD.

- Illustrate a story.

- Write a story.

- Make a picture and write about it.

- Type my spelling words.

- Edit a piece of my writing.

- Research an author.

- Read a book review online.

- Write a book review and post it online.

- E-mail a pen pal.

- Use Accelerated Reader.

Troubleshooting

The following table lists possible problems you might encounter at the computer work station and how you might troubleshoot them with your class.

Computer Work Station

Possible Problem	Troubleshooting Ideas
Everyone wants a turn.	To answer the question "When do I get to go to the computers?" have a sheet posted by this station that shows each child's name and when that child gets to go to the station (see Figure 9.1). Try not to pull students for guided reading when they are scheduled for the computer.
Children get too loud.	You might try removing the headsets and teaching children to keep the volume at a low level. Students often can't monitor their voices at this station because they can't hear themselves.
Children interrupt the teacher because they need help.	Be sure students know how to play the games or use the program ahead of time. Have a "computer expert" to help children who require assistance so you don't have to run to the rescue constantly. (Appendix H has badges you can use to indicate which student is filling this role.) Some teachers put a red plastic cup at each computer. When students need help, they simply place the cup on top of the computer as a signal for someone to help them.
Students play the same game over and over.	Have several games available and tell students you expect them to play a certain number or certain ones. If a game is overused, you might choose to remove it for a while to make students try something else.
Children just draw. No reading and writing is taking place.	Take away the option of the drawing program and replace it with more literacy-related activities, such as reading a book on a CD or playing a literacy game.
This game is just a glorified worksheet.	Choose computer games wisely. Be sure that they challenge children to think. Offer students a variety of literacy-related activities at the computer. Don't rely solely on games for literacy practice.
My students constantly interrupt me to take an Accelerated Reader test.	Let children do their Accelerated Reader tests on their assigned day for the computer work station. Let them use their book when taking the test in case they finished the book several days earlier. Remember that when children take standardized tests, they can look back in the passage to answer questions!

Listening Work Station

Two children sit in a quiet spot listening to a tape of a favorite read-aloud book. Their teacher made this audiotape during read-aloud time. The children love listening to her voice and to their classmates' comments on the tape. They turn the pages at the sound of the bell (the teacher had a student ring a bell each time she turned a page). When the chil-

Figure 9.1 Weekly Computer Schedule

Monday	Leticia Morgan	Samuel Nanci	Ben Adam
Tuesday	Joni Miguel	Tony Phillip	Madison Noe
Wednesday	Danielle Marcus	Jill	Mark
Thursday	Tania Natalie	Billi	Kaan
Friday	Lillian Leah	Shiquitta	Terrence

dren have finished listening, they rewind the tape and talk about their favorite parts. If there is time, they may write about or illustrate an event from the book they just listened to.

Ideas for the Work Station

The listening work station is one of the easiest to establish in the classroom. All you need is a tape recorder and some books with matching audiotapes. Many commercially produced children's books on tape are available, which makes setup that much easier.

Find a comfortable place for children to sit for your listening work station. Some teachers use beanbag chairs or pillows to define this space. Others let students take the materials back to their desks if floor space is limited. Some teachers opt to use a Walkman type of tape recorder with batteries so each child can have his or her own book and tape. Inexpensive models are available at many drugstores. They usually use AA batteries, which you might ask parents or community members to donate.

The main thing children do at this station is listen to tapes. Provide a variety of material for them to listen to: nonfiction books, magazine excerpts, newspaper articles, music, poems, and stories. Sometimes let them just listen for entertainment. Other times you might set a purpose for listening. You might also have them write a response after listening to a tape. For a change of pace, convert your listening work station into a recording studio, where students can record their own reading and make tapes.

Here are some things that you might include on the "I Can" list at this station:

A listening work station in an inviting corner, made from a breakfast tray and child-sized beach chairs.

A listening work station storage table made from a popcorn tin with ply board at the top; books and tapes are stored inside.

I can . . .

- Turn the page with the beep.

- Read along with the book.

- Talk to my partner about the tape when we're finished listening.

- Draw a picture of my favorite part of the tape.

- Write about something I learned by listening today.

- Retell the story I heard today.

Troubleshooting

There are quite a number of things that can cause trouble at this station. The best way to avoid these is to model well and reteach as needed. Interestingly, you may notice that removing the headphones is one way to avoid a variety of problems.

Directions written by the class help solve problems at the listening work station.

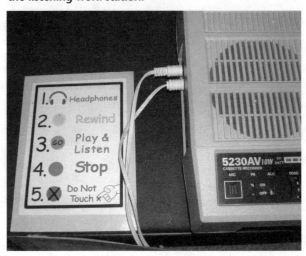

Listening Work Station

Possible Problem	Troubleshooting Ideas
Some students make the volume too loud.	Try doing without the headphones. This way the children and you can monitor the noise level. Or try presetting the volume and putting tape over it.
Children get too loud.	Again, remove the headphones. It's often hard for children to monitor their voice level with these on.
Children interrupt the teacher because they need help with the equipment (headsets don't work, tape isn't rewound, etc.).	Be sure students know how to use the equipment ahead of time. Have a "tape rewinder" who can help others rewind or restart a tape if children have trouble. If the headsets give you trouble, just remove them.
Students play with the plug.	Use portable Walkman-type tape recorders instead of the traditional ones. No plug is needed!
Children have erased some of the tapes.	Remove little plastic pieces from the top of the cassette tape, and the tape becomes unerasable.

Puzzles and Games Work Station

In one classroom there are four children at the puzzles and games work station. Two are playing a game and two are working on a puzzle together. They are sitting on a carpeted area beside some shelves that hold several other puzzles and games. One shelf is labeled "Puzzles"; another, "Games." The teacher has chosen not to display every puzzle and game she owns, because she knows that would be too many pieces for students to manage.

The children are chatting quietly as they work on their zoo animal puzzle. "Let's do the border first, like Mrs. Terry showed us," one says. "Here's a corner piece. Ooh, this is going to be a tiger. I love seeing their striped fur at the zoo." These students are solving problems cooperatively as they work. They are also using expressive language to talk about the content of the puzzle.

The two others are playing checkers, a game that some of the children have played at home. When their teacher taught them how to play checkers, the class wrote a how-to piece about this game. It is typed and available for them to read at this station if they need help with the rules. If they get stuck, the players read the chart together. If they finish playing one game, they can play it again. Or they might choose to move on to Chutes and Ladders, another game their teacher has demonstrated for them.

Ideas for the Work Station

The puzzles and games work station is another relatively easy station to open at the beginning of the school year. Teachers sometimes use it as a temporary station until they have other literacy work stations established in their classrooms. Then they substitute another work station with more literacy possibilities for this one.

You can send more than two students to this station at a time, or you can separate it into two different stations, one for puzzles and the other for games. If space is a problem in your classroom, children can take the materials back to their seats or to a table to work on them.

If you have a puzzles and games work station later in the year, you might teach children how to make their own puzzles or games. There are blank puzzles available online (try www.blankbooks.com) as well as through commercial publishers. You might do a search on the Internet by typing in "blank puzzles" to locate sources for making your own puzzles. Games are easily made with manila folders, spinners, or dice. The Ellison Company also makes dies for puzzles and games. These are available at www.ellison.com.

Following is an "I Can" list of some things children can do at the puzzles and games station. You might choose to list the names of the games or puzzles that you have available for children to use.

I can . . .

- Put a puzzle together (horses, zoo animals, covered bridge).

- Play a game (checkers, Chutes and Ladders).

- Cooperate with my partner.

- Count the pieces in a puzzle to be sure I have all I need.

- Write a note if pieces are missing.

- Make my own puzzle.

- Make my own game.

Troubleshooting

Use the chart on the next page to think about what to model so children can solve their own problems as they arise.

Puzzles and Games Work Station

Possible Problem	Troubleshooting Ideas
Children have trouble taking turns.	Model how to take turns. See the section in Chapter 2 "Mini-Lessons at the Beginning of the School Year."
Students are not finished when it's time to switch work stations.	You might want to let children finish playing their game if they are near the end of it. Tell the others coming to this station to play a different game. If space is limited, tell the students coming to this station to take their game to their desk. If children haven't finished a puzzle, they might let the next group add on to it.
Pieces are missing.	Provide sticky notes and have children write a note telling specifically what is missing. Have them put the puzzle or game in a box labeled "Missing Pieces." Have the materials manager take care of the repairs.
Students aren't cleaning up well.	Be sure you don't have too many materials displayed at this work station, or cleanup may be difficult. Adding labels to containers will help. You may have to have students practice cleaning up (instead of playing) if this becomes a consistent problem.
There's not enough room for me to put this station in my classroom.	Let some children work on puzzles and games at their desks. Keep materials in a labeled tub that can easily be carried to another location in your classroom.

Storing puzzles and games on labeled shelves helps keep materials neat.

Buddy Reading Work Station

A pair of students sit beside each other. Each holds a copy of the same book. In a kindergarten classroom it may be two small copies of a Big Book they read together in shared reading a few weeks earlier. In first grade, it might be two copies of an easy book their teacher read aloud to them several days before. In second grade, it may be two copies of their social studies textbook, with a bookmark at the part that was discussed in class the day before.

The children take turns reading in a variety of ways the teacher has modeled. They may read the whole piece together in unison, then take turns with one reading one page and the other reading the next. Or one may read the whole book aloud, then the other reads it again. It is up to the children to decide how to read it. The only rule is that they read the same book together. After they read, they might talk about their favorite parts. "How about I read a page, and then you read a page? I like that kind of buddy reading," says Michael to his partner. "Okay," responds Lynda. "You go first."

Ideas for the Work Station

The buddy reading work station usually goes well once students have been introduced to some books they can read easily. It is easy to establish this work station at the start of second grade, but it will take some time in kindergarten. All you need for materials is a small tub or basket with two identical copies of several titles in it. You might add colored dots that correspond with the children's reading group to help them find books that are just right for them. For example, you can tell the students in the red reading group to be sure to pick books with red dots at buddy reading. This will help them find books that are at an appropriate reading level.

Model for children a variety of ways to do buddy reading and post these at an "I Can" list as you introduce them.

> **I can . . .**

■ Read a book with my buddy.

■ Read a page, then you read a page.

■ Read a page, then you be my echo.

■ Read the whole book, then you read the whole book.

■ Read a character's part, then you read another character's part.

■ Read a social studies chapter with my buddy.

Troubleshooting

The biggest challenge at this work station is how to keep buddy reading fresh and interesting. Here are a few ways:

Buddy reading visors add novelty as two children read the same book together.

Buddy reading glasses keep this work station fun and interesting.

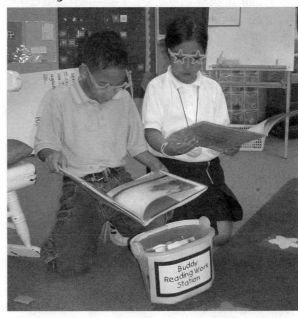

An inflatable child's wading pool holds two child-sized pillows for buddy reading.

- Add new books over time.

- Remove books that children have grown tired of.

- Add special buddy reading badges and buddy reading pointers designed by the children.

- Add two pairs of matching sunglasses from a dollar store with the lenses removed and call them buddy reading glasses.

- Add two oversized white T-shirts labeled "Buddy Reading." Let the children decorate them with titles of favorite books read during buddy reading.

Be sure not to add all these items at once. Add one new item at a time, as you see that this work station needs a boost. If children get tired of buddy reading, remove the station altogether and reintroduce it later in the year.

Overhead Work Station

The kindergarten teacher places her overhead on the floor. It projects onto a large dry-erase board.

Two children place a short poem typed in large print on a transparency onto the overhead. They project the print onto the board and use pointers as they read the poem together. It's a familiar poem, one that they've read together many times in shared reading. After they read it, they circle and read the words they know with a dry-erase marker on the board. Then they erase the board and read another poem.

In a first-grade classroom, two children use magnetic letters on the overhead to make their spelling words. Then they sort overhead word tiles from a commercial publisher. They put two-letter words in one row and three-letter words in another. They read the words together and use some of them to make a sentence. One child writes his sentence on a strip of paper provided at this station and puts it in his work station folder to discuss during sharing time.

At the overhead work station in a second-grade classroom, a pair of students are projecting a transparency onto a screen just as their teacher did during their daily Morning Message time. She had written the class a letter on the transparency telling about their day and had omitted words and parts of words and left blanks in their place (see Figure 9.2). Then she put the letter in a clear plastic sleeve. The class read the message together and took turns coming up to the overhead and filling in the blanks with missing letters. They used a thin dry-erase pen,

Figure 9.2 Morning Message

> Novemb_ _ 20, 2002
>
> Good Morn_ _ _, Boys and G_ _rls,
>
>   Today we will be study_ _ _ about health_ foods. Wh_ _ did you eat for breakfast to_ _ _? Make a list of the foods you ate. Put a ☆ beside each healthy food on your list.
>
> Your teacher,
>
> Mrs. Diller

A three-ring notebook holds transparencies in clear plastic sleeves, sorted into categories, such as poems, morning messages, and handwriting.

Making spelling words with magnetic letters on the overhead projector at the overhead work station.

so no water was necessary to erase the letters. They simply wiped the plastic clean with their fingers. Now these two children are doing exactly what their teacher modeled earlier.

Ideas for the Work Station

When setting up the overhead work station, place the overhead low enough so students can easily access it. Some kindergarten and first-grade teachers put it on the floor or on a low, flat board on wheels, like a rolling plant stand. Others put the overhead on a low rolling cart so it can easily be moved around the room. Still others might keep the overhead on a spare student desk.

Be sure all materials students will need for the overhead are at their fingertips so they don't have to interrupt you or anyone else. You might store transparencies you have used during instruction in a three-ring notebook with sections labeled appropriately—"Poems," "Morning Messages," "Handwriting," "Reading Lessons," and so on. Put each transparency in a clear plastic sleeve for protection and easy storage. Or you might place transparencies in a file folder, taped on the sides to create a pouch, and attach this to the overhead with Velcro or tape. (A cover graphic, "Things to Use on the Overhead," is provided in Appendix H.) Include several small pointers in a labeled cup, and have a few thin dry-erase pens handy in another labeled container. Some teachers like to store overhead materials in an overhead caddy that attaches to the machine with

Velcro. This caddy is available through many educational publishers, such as the Teaching Resource Center at www.trcabc.com.

Children can do a variety of activities for practice at the overhead work station. They can work with any transparency you have used in class. Here are some ideas for an "I Can" list:

I can . . .

■ Read a poem on a transparency.

■ Circle and read special words in a poem.

■ Make words with magnetic letters.

■ Make words with overhead letter tiles.

■ Make sentences with overhead word tiles.

■ Sort and read overhead word tiles.

■ Read and complete a transparency my teacher did with us in class.

■ Read and complete a Morning Message on a transparency.

■ Practice handwriting on the overhead.

Troubleshooting

Here is a table listing possible problems you might encounter at this work station, with ideas for solving them.

Pocket Chart Work Station

At the beginning of the year, the teacher introduces the students' names to the class, one at a time, and places each name in a pocket chart. She also takes each child's photo with a camera (digital and Polaroid cameras give immediate results) and places these in the pocket chart, too. Now, at the pocket chart work station, two students choose from a variety of tasks to do with the cards during independent work time. They can match the names and photos; they can sort and read boys' names and girls' names; they can put the names in alphabetical order.

As the teacher introduces poems in shared reading, she copies some of them line by line onto sentence strips and adds these to the pocket chart station. Later, during work station time, pairs of students work together to put the lines in order and practice reading the poems fluently. They search for special kinds of words and circle them with Wikki Stix, a favorite tool, just as their teacher did with them in class.

Later in the year, the same teacher reads a book aloud and the class does a shared writing of the main events from the story, putting each event on a separate sentence strip. These are then placed at the pocket chart station for sequencing. After this activity has been modeled several times, some chil-

Overhead Work Station

Possible Problem	Troubleshooting Ideas
Children have trouble sharing materials.	Limit the number of students at this work station to two.
Students fight over who turns the machine on and off.	Teach children that one will turn it on and the other will turn it off.
The water spray bottle makes a mess with the vis-à-vis pens.	Substitute dry-erase markers for vis-à-vis pens. Use transparencies in clear plastic sleeves. For easiest cleanup, erase transparencies within about ten minutes of use.
I'm afraid the children might break the overhead.	Teach students exactly how to use this machine, just as you do with the computer and the tape recorder.

A pocket chart work station set up on a bulletin board low enough for children to reach it.

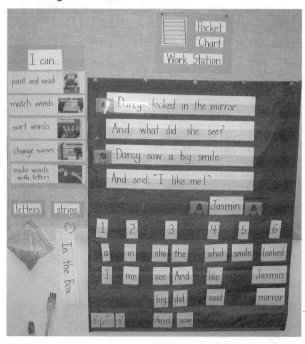

A poem is written line by line on sentence strips, color-coded on the back, and fastened together by a metal book ring.

dren take other read-aloud books and create their own set of sequencing cards to go with these familiar stories. When children come to the pocket chart work station, they enjoy putting these cards in order to retell books they know.

Ideas for the Work Station

All you need to set up this work station is a pocket chart hung on a wall or stand and a place to store materials. You might keep sentence strips in a plastic wallpaper tray (available at hardware stores). Lakeshore (www.lakeshore.com) also makes a wooden tray for sentence strip storage. One easy management tip is to put a matching colored dot on the back of each sentence strip in a set. Hole-punch each strip on the end and fasten a set together with a one-inch metal book ring. You might include the matching poem on a small card with a matching colored dot on back, so students can self-check their work. Small cards might be

stored in labeled zip-lock bags. Color-coding the cards may also be helpful for student management.

Multitudes of children's poetry books are available through your school and public libraries. Publishers such as Scholastic carry many poems for specific grade levels. My own book *Beyond the Names Chart: Using Children's Names for Word Study* (2002) includes poems with children's names, which is a good way to open up your pocket chart work station. Use these resources to create sentence strip poems. For handwriting practice, let some of your students make these for you. And include some laminated blank sentence strips and markers that students can use again and again.

There are three main categories of things students can do at the pocket chart work station: they can *match, sort,* and *sequence.* See the "I Can" list below for ideas in each category.

For matching:

I can match . . .

- Names and photos.
- Names and missing letters.
- Words and pictures.
- Words and definitions.
- Individual words to those in a poem written on sentence strips.
- Words with similar meanings (synonyms).
- Words with opposite meanings (antonyms).

For sorting:

I can sort . . .

- Pictures.
- Letters by features.
- Letters with different fonts.
- Names (boys and girls, number of letters, same first letter, number of syllables, etc.).

Emergent readers practice one-to-one matching by pointing to and reading each word in a poem.

Two girls sort words from the poem by the number of letters and then point and read the word sort.

- Words (number of letters, short vowel pattern, long vowel pattern, number of syllables, etc.).
- Rhyming words.

For sequencing:

I can sequence . . .

- Lines in a poem.
- Events of a story (told in pictures or sentences).
- Words in ABC order.
- Things that happened in a science experiment.
- Directions to follow.
- Words to create my own sentence.
- Words to create my own poem.

Troubleshooting

The table on the next page lists possible problems you might encounter at this work station, with ideas for solving them.

I have, unfortunately, seen many teachers close down this station because students were off-task.

Pocket Chart Work Station

Possible Problem	Troubleshooting Ideas
There are so many materials. What a mess!	Have a good storage system. Color-code items in a set. Have a labeled place for everything. Don't put out too many materials at once.
My students get easily bored at this station.	Limit the number of materials available at once. Provide maybe a maximum of four or five tasks to choose from. Vary these every few weeks to keep things fresh. Get student input on what they'd like to do at this work station. Bring back old materials, such as their names, later in the year. Children love to look at their names and photos, no matter what age they are!

Before you give up on this work station, check to see why children aren't behaving. Perhaps they are bored with the activities, or they don't know what to do. Always reteach before abandoning a station. Or consider closing this work station for some of the year. You might use it for a month or so, and then reintroduce it periodically later in the year as a special station.

Creation Work Station

A first-grade class has been studying the art of Lois Ehlert. They love the books by this wonderful author and illustrator that their teacher has read aloud to them. Ehlert's bold colors and shapes appeal to young readers. The teacher has just finished reading *Under My Nose,* Lois Ehlert's autobiography, and has placed it at the creation work station along with a tub of Ehlert's picture books and art supplies for the students to use in making collages, Ehlert's favorite technique. The class has written a set of directions on how to make a collage, and it is posted at the work station.

Two children eagerly move into this station. They read the "I Can" list together. "What do you want to do? Let's see. I can read about Lois Ehlert, look at her books and study her craft, make a col-

lage, or make illustrations to go with a book I've written." They decide to look at some of her books and then work together to make a collage. As they revisit some of Ehlert's books, they discuss patterns they notice. "She uses a lot of bright colors. She makes lots of pictures of stuff from nature. Let's make an animal with colored shapes. Let's use her book *Color Zoo* for ideas. I like the tiger. We'll need a white circle to start . . ."

Creation work station highlighting Lois Ehlert, illustrator and children's book author.

These children are using literacy and art to express themselves. They will begin their project today. If they don't finish it, they might choose to take the work to their seats and continue there instead of going to the next place on the work station management board. Or they might store their project in their work station folder and come back to it another day or during free time.

Ideas for the Work Station

The creation work station takes the place of an art center, and it is designed to combine literacy and art. Students come to this station to create artwork related to books they have read and written. They also read and write about artists at this station. Materials are organized in labeled containers so students can find them easily. There are directions for making a variety of art products, as well as resource books to help students draw and create.

Here are some ideas for an "I Can" list in this work station:

I can . . .

- Read about an artist.

- Read about an illustrator.

- Study illustrations in books by the same illustrator and look for patterns.

- Make a puppet for a play I read.

- Make puppets for a play I wrote.

- Illustrate a book I wrote.

- Illustrate a story I wrote.

- Make props to go with a play I read.

- Make a mask to go with a favorite character from a book I read.

- Design a book jacket for a book I read.

- Read and follow directions to make something.

- Read a book about how to make something.

- Read a how-to-draw book and make a drawing.

Troubleshooting

The table on the next page lists possible problems you might encounter at this work station, with ideas for solving them.

Science/Social Studies Work Station

Lisbeth and Mario are in the science work station. Their class has been studying about plants. The "I Can" list posted at the station shows a variety of things they might do related to this unit of study. For example, they can read a book about plants, write and illustrate a five-page book about plants, put together a plant puzzle the class has created, or measure the plants growing in the pots on the science table and write their observations in their science log. Lisbeth decides to make a book, while Mario works on the plant puzzle. When Mario is

Artifacts, books, and magnifying glasses in a science work station focused on a study of rocks.

Creation Work Station

Possible Problem	Troubleshooting Ideas
I don't have room for this in my classroom. Help!	You might use low shelves inside a cabinet to store the materials for this station. Post your "I Can" list and any directions on the inside of the cabinet doors. Simply have children open the cabinet doors and take materials needed back to their seats to work. Or place materials in a labeled tub with the "I Can" list and any directions on sheets inside the tub and let students take this portable station to their desks.
My students are taking too many materials at once and there's nothing left for the others.	Limit the number of materials available at a time. Tell children that they can make only one of something—one book, one puppet, one mask, etc. Explain the need to have enough materials for everyone to make something.
Can't I just put this in my writing work station?	Of course you can. However, if you see children spending all their time drawing and little or no time writing, you might want to have two separate stations as suggested here.
My class makes a mess at this station and doesn't clean up well.	Again, limit the number of materials for easier cleanup. Be sure to have labeled containers for all materials to help the area stay organized. Get children to help make the labels to promote ownership. Have students end a bit early at this station if they need more time for cleanup.
Students don't want to go to any other work station. This is their favorite. I'm afraid they're not doing enough reading and writing.	It is wonderful when children find something they love to do, but you certainly want to be sure they're getting enough reading and writing practice. Tell students that they must read or write something to go with the product they are making at this station. Then follow up! Have them bring their reading, writing, and related art to sharing time. This will provide a good model for the rest of the class as well.

finished, he reads a book about plants. He reads a favorite part to Lisbeth. When she completes her homemade plant book, she shares it with Mario. He says he thinks he will make his own plant book next time he comes here.

In another classroom, several children are at the social studies work station. They too are engaged in a unit of study, and the activities here relate to it. They are learning about maps. One tub holds maps of local places; another tub holds atlases; a third houses picture books that contain maps. Also at the station is a commercially made puzzle of the United States and a homemade puzzle of a map of the school. There are copies of a United States map and colored pencils available for children to map places they have visited. The "I Can" list, which the class composed together, gives the children several choices of activities. They could, for example, look carefully at the maps and make a list of what they notice about them; do a map puzzle and notice what is included on the map; make a map of their classroom; read a book about maps; take a U.S. map and note places they have visited; write about a place they have visited and show its location on the map; work with a map and write directions for how to travel someplace, using the words *north, south, east,* and *west.*

Ideas for the Work Station

An area can be set up for either social studies or science, or the two might be combined into one work station. The activities and materials at this work station will change periodically as your class explores new topics of study in the content areas. You might post a chart here entitled "What We're Learning About" with the topics noted (water, the solar system, national patriotic holidays, whatever). Have students add to the list as they learn new information while reading and writing at this station. Include a tub of books related to the unit. Have available paper and pencils for students to write about what they learned. You might include blank books (four or five pieces of blank paper stapled together) for students to use to make their own books about the topic. Also have a place for artifacts related to the unit. You might call it "Our Museum" and have children label the items displayed. For example, you might have a collection of rocks or pictures of famous heroes being studied.

The "I Can" lists at this station will change depending on the unit of study and will probably be more specific than those at other work stations, since particular topics are targeted here. The following are examples.

For a kindergarten study of pets:

I can . . .

- Read books about pets.

- Draw a picture of a pet and write about what a pet needs.

- Sort pictures of pets.

- Tell about my sort.

- Do a pet survey.

For a first-grade study of insects:

I can . . .

- Read about insects.

- Make and label an insect diagram.

- Write five facts about insects.

- Choose one insect and make a poster about it.

- Use a magnifying lens to observe an insect in the jar.

- Write about what I observe on a clipboard.

For a second-grade study of citizenship:

I can . . .

- Read a book and tell what made the character a good citizen (give examples of truth, equality, justice).

- Write about a time someone I know showed good citizenship.

- Write a letter to someone who has shown good citizenship and thank that person for his or her example.

- Listen to or sing a patriotic song.

- Read about state and national symbols.

- Read a brochure about my state.

- Make a brochure about state and national symbols.

Troubleshooting

Here is a table listing possible problems you might encounter at this work station, with ideas for solving them.

Science/Social Studies Work Station

Possible Problem	Troubleshooting Ideas
I tried to assign a product, but students couldn't make the brochure (poster or whatever) on their own.	Model doing several examples of one product together as a class before you ask children to create a product independently. Look at real-world examples, too. For example, if you want students to make a brochure, make brochures together. Then include sample brochures at this station along with prefolded paper.
Children can't read the content-area books I put at this station. They are too hard.	Ask your librarian or reading specialist to help you obtain books written at easier levels. Several publishers specialize in nonfiction books for young readers. You might check out Benchmark Education (www.benchmarkeducation .com, Heinemann Classroom (www.heinemannclassroom .com), or Newbridge (www.newbridgeonline.com) for possibilities.

Handwriting Work Station

Handwriting instruction is important because children benefit from having neat, fluent writing that others can easily read. Children need clear teaching on how to form letters. In this first-grade classroom the teacher demonstrates correct letter formation during modeled writing as he writes in front of his

A handwriting work station set up near a chalkboard for practice.

class, and he reinforces his teaching doing interactive writing, sharing the pen with the children. He also has scheduled lessons where he models correct letter formation for the whole class. The children sometimes sing letter songs as they write letters in the air and practice with big gestures using their whole arm before moving to pencil and paper.

However, instead of spending fifteen to twenty minutes a day for whole-class handwriting instruction, the teacher allows children to practice at the handwriting work station. He also observes them as they write pieces during their scheduled time for writing. There is limited space in this classroom, so the teacher has set up his handwriting work station essentially in a plastic tub. In it he has placed a variety of materials for handwriting practice: ruled paper, pencils, letter formation cards, blank paper, letter templates for tracing, and a dry-erase flip book that he found in the toy section of the local Wal-Mart.

Two children come to this station at a time and take the tub back to their desks. They sit beside each other, write a bit, and then check each other's handwriting. "I think that's the best *g* you wrote," one says to the other. "It sits on the line and is easy to read." The children continue to discuss their work as they write, using precisely the language they heard their teacher use when he looked at their writing the other day. They are following their teacher's model and using his words to help each other.

Ideas for the Work Station

The handwriting work station is very simple to set up. It doesn't take much space or preparation time. Here are some things students might put on an "I Can" list for this station:

I can . . .

- Practice writing letters with a pencil.
- Practice writing letters with a pen.
- Circle my best letter and tell why it's the best.
- Use a dry-erase pen on the practice board.

- Write letters with my finger in the sand tray.
- Copy a poem for handwriting practice.
- Teach my partner how to make a letter.
- Use the stencils and trace letters.
- Trace a letter over and over again in different colors to make a rainbow letter.
- Use letter formation cards.

Troubleshooting

Below is a table listing possible problems you might encounter at this work station, with ideas for solving them.

This chapter presented a wide variety of additional literacy work stations that might be used in your classroom throughout the year. You will most likely never have all of these up and running at once. Consider the ideas in this chapter a menu of possibilities from which you might choose.

Handwriting Work Station

Possible Problem	**Troubleshooting Ideas**
Students are practicing incorrect letter formation.	Try modeling again. You may also have to sit beside some of these children as they practice. Or find another child to tutor them at this station.
The children's handwriting practice is sloppy. I don't think this station is working.	Add some more meaningful tasks for them to do at this station. Perhaps you need a new sign for a tub of books at the classroom library. Or you need a letter copied to send to the principal. Giving children a sense of audience may help them improve their practice.
I'm seeing lots of off-task behavior here.	Try to figure out what is causing the trouble. If boredom seems to be the reason, add something new at this station to generate renewed interest. For example, get some gel pens and black paper. Or copy handwriting paper onto pastel-colored paper and provide colored pencils. If a child has poor fine motor control, add some tasks to improve fine motor skills, such as making letters with play dough or picking up pasta letters with tweezers to spell words.

Special Notes for Kindergarten Teachers

If you teach kindergarten, you might already use some of the work stations mentioned in this chapter. You might call them by different names or have slightly different materials in them, but most likely you have already tried some of these. You probably also start your year with traditional kindergarten centers, such as housekeeping, blocks, and a sand or water table. Many kindergarten teachers add the literacy work stations throughout the year as they introduce more and more print to students through reading aloud, shared reading, modeled writing, interactive writing, and word wall lessons.

How to Add Literacy to Traditional Kindergarten Centers

As I work with educators across the country, some kindergarten teachers tell me that well-meaning administrators who don't fully understand the value of play to develop language and literacy concepts are removing their housekeeping and block centers. I believe that kindergarten teachers have a responsibility to add more literacy to these traditional centers so that children can keep their time-honored right to play as they learn. Here are some ways to add more reading and writing to three of your traditional kindergarten centers.

Housekeeping Center

As I visit pre-kindergarten and kindergarten classrooms, I'm sometimes surprised by the lack of materials for reading and writing in the housekeeping center. It is fairly easy to add such materials. Just think about the kinds of real-life reading and writing you do at home and add those materials to the center gradually. (Don't put them all out at once or children may not pay attention to

Print-rich opportunities abound at the housekeeping center in kindergarten.

them.) You may also need to sit down with the children and show them how to use these new items as they play.

Here's a list of some possibilities for the housekeeping center:

- Simple recipes (with pictures and a few words). Maybe use them to prepare snacks before placing them in the housekeeping center.

- Children's cookbooks.

- A telephone book (homemade, with each page featuring one child's name, a photo of the child, and the child's phone number).

- An address book (homemade, with each page featuring one child's name, a photo, and the child's address).

- Telephone numbers for local restaurants and stores children know (homemade, with each page featuring a logo and some environmental print and a phone number, such as the name "McDonald's" with the corresponding logo and phone number).

- Order pads (for a restaurant theme).

- Message pads by the telephone.

- List paper for writing grocery lists.

- Grocery ads for writing grocery lists.

- Store ads.

- Toy catalogs.

- Magazines.

- TV listings.

- A newspaper section on movies.

- A message board (dry erase).

- Envelopes.

- Postcards.

- Play money.

- A play telephone.

Throughout the year consider changing this area into a variety of play stations (with related literacy materials), such as the following:

- Doctor's offices (pediatrician, vet, dentist, optometrist).

- A post office.

- A restaurant (Pizza Hut, Wendy's . . .).

- A place for birthday parties.

- A school.

- An office.

- The beach.

- A grocery store.

- A farm market.

- A flower shop.

- A garden center.

- A museum.

Block Center

Boys and girls enjoy building with blocks. As they do so they use problem-solving and mathematical skills. It is a bit more challenging to add literacy activities to the block area, but it can be done. Again, add items gradually. Also, sit with the children and play with them to help them use more elaborate and cooperative oral language as they build things with blocks. Here are some ways to add literacy at this station:

- Provide a road map rug in this area.

- Include maps of your city or state.

- Hang a world map nearby and talk about places on it.

Make the kindergarten block center print-rich by adding maps, labels, and building cards.

Road signs add literacy activities to the kindergarten block center.

- Include picture books that show homes in other countries and help students try to build homes like these.

- Provide architectural books, floor plans, and blueprints of houses and other buildings (from decorating magazines, the Internet, builders, or real estate agents).

- Provide environmental print signs for stores, restaurants, and streets (homemade, with Tinker Toys or Popsicle sticks and environmental print).

- Help children make labels for their buildings.

- Take digital photos of their buildings and put them in a teacher-made book that is kept at this center.

- Help children spell their names or other words with blocks.

- Tape environmental print onto small blocks to represent buildings.

Sand or Water Center

Finally, consider literacy possibilities at the sand or water center. Here are a few ideas:

- Use plastic letters, numbers, and animal molds for sand play.

- Put ABC confetti in a bit of water and let children catch letters with a plastic spoon and name the letters.

- Fill a tray with shaving cream and let children practice writing their names and high-frequency words in it.

- Use ABC cookie cutters pressed into sand to form names and other words.

- Put alphabet pasta in the sand tray for a change.

- Let children use letter sponges in water.

- Partially fill plastic tubs with sand and let children write in them.

- Have a piece of shower board (available from a home supply store) and let students write with bathtub soap crayons that can be washed off with water.

- Bury magnetic or foam letters in sand and have children dig for them in a "treasure hunt."

Reflection and Dialogue

Consider the following:

1. What helped you most in this chapter? Which ideas were most useful to you?
2. Which of the work stations from this chapter do you already have in your classroom? What's working well with them? What would you like to change? Discuss your ideas with your team.
3. Which of the work stations in this chapter would you like to add to your classroom? Share several ideas with a colleague. (Keep in mind that this chapter includes more choices

than you would probably want to use in your classroom at one time.)

4. How do you schedule students to use the computer in your classroom? How have you maximized computer use? Talk with someone about your ideas.

5. Choose a new work station from this chapter. Work with a partner to plan a mini-lesson for introducing it to your class.

6. If you have (or plan to have) a puzzles and games work station (or substitute a different work station or even a kindergarten center), practice telling another teacher how it supports literacy development at your grade level. Be prepared in case a parent or an administrator asks you this. Always have a rationale for all the activities at literacy work stations and traditional kindergarten centers!

7. Choose any work station from this chapter. Make a "novelty plan" for how to keep it fresh and interesting over the next six weeks. Remember, you don't have to change everything on Fridays.

8. If you teach kindergarten, discuss ways you have already added literacy to your traditional centers, and share new ideas you plan to try. Visit other kindergarten classrooms and talk with the teachers so that you may help each other increase the opportunities for literacy at centers.

Planning for Practice at Literacy Work Stations

How do I plan literacy work stations that meet the needs of all the students in my class? Once you have your stations up and running and have learned to manage them, this is the question you may ask. The best place to begin planning is to look at what your students already know how to do and then think about what they need next. You can get this information from running records and students' writing samples. You can also keep anecdotal notes about what children do as readers and writers as you watch them throughout the day. Another source of information is other types of written work that students do at school.

In order to collect this data, you need to schedule time in your day to watch and reflect on what you see students doing. This is best accomplished if you are meeting with about two groups a day. Some teachers feel pressured to work with every one of their small reading groups daily, but if you are trying to work with four or five groups a day, you will not have time to be reflective. Quality, not quantity, is the name of the game with small-group instruction.

As you read this chapter, try one thing at a time. Don't try to do it all at once, or you will probably end up feeling overwhelmed. Read through the chapter and highlight ideas that interest you. Then look at the corresponding activities in the "Reflection and Dialogue" section at the end of the chapter. Choose an activity that matches an idea that you would like to try. Work with a colleague for support. Take one bit at a time and layer on new pieces as you feel comfortable. You might want to begin by using the assessment and planning activities for your students who are struggling the most. This will make the task more manageable and will probably yield the biggest results for your time invested.

Using a Clipboard

Many teachers have found that carrying a clipboard around the classroom helps them record their observations, which in turns aids planning. Index cards can be useful for this. Begin by writing each

A clipboard with an index card for each child taped onto it can be useful in assessment.

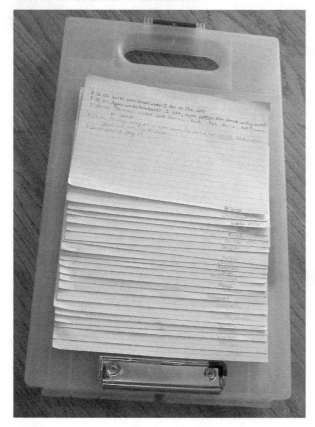

child's name on the bottom right-hand side of a card. Prepare a card for each student. Then, tape the first card to the clipboard so it is aligned with the bottom of the clipboard. Layer the second card over the first, so that the first name as well as the second child's name is visible. Continue taping cards to the clipboard until all are attached, with each child's name showing.

During work station time, walk around the classroom and jot down notes about individual children's literacy behavior. Be sure to date each entry and keep it brief. You will have to schedule time for observation before or after a guided reading group, at least twice a month. You can also make observations while working with students during small-group reading instruction or during independent writing time. You may feel more successful if you begin by

observing the students you are most puzzled about, the ones you're least sure about how to help.

Here are some examples of things you might record:

- Self-corrected one-to-one match.

- Reread for meaning.

- Tried first sound and used picture.

- Skipped word and read on, then returned and fixed.

- Used beginning and ending sounds of unknown words.

- Self-corrected punctuation when rereading.

- Chose just-right book on snakes.

- Flipped through page; no oral language used.

- Talked about book with friend after reading.

- Drew picture; mock letters.

- Used word wall for spelling high-frequency words *was, like.*

- Asked friend for help with spelling.

- Chose writing topic quickly and easily.

- Needed help segmenting words to write them.

- Joined most sentences with *and.*

- Wrote, then drew picture.

After a child's card is full, simply tear it off and put it in the child's folder. Then replace it with a new card so you can continue to take notes throughout the year.

Running Records

Running records contain valuable information that can be used for planning for students at work stations. You might begin by looking at one guided reading group's running records at a time. The records don't all have to pertain to the same book. Just look across the running records for that one group taken over the course of a week or two. What do you notice? Look for patterns across the records. For example, what are students paying attention to visually? Do they use only the beginning sounds of new words, or are they considering just beginning and ending sounds and neglecting the middle of words? Are they able to use blends, digraphs, and diphthongs? Do they confuse long and short vowels? Do they get stuck on multi-syllabic words? Jot down your observations on a planning sheet, such as the one in Appendix I. See Figure 10.1 for an example of a completed planning sheet.

Examine how children use structural cues while they read, or how their reading sounds. Does what they read sound right in English? Or are they, for example, reading *seed* for *saw* (a grammatical error)?

Are they leaving off endings? Are bilingual students switching the order of adjectives and nouns (because that's the grammatical structure of their native language)? All of these questions will help you find ways to help your students with the structural system of language (or grammar).

Look at meaning cues, too. Are children using pictures to help them read? Are they using pictures and words together and self-checking between the two? Does their reading make sense? Are they using the story line to guide their predictions? Do children make up and substitute words that don't make sense?

Now check to see if the children are using more than one of these three—visual, structural, meaning—cuing systems. Do they cross-check from one source of information to another? For example, do they use the story line to make a prediction of a word and then check the word to be sure it looks like their prediction? Do they read a

Figure 10.1 Running Records Sheet

Looking at Patterns in Running Records			
Group Blue Date 10-17-02			
Child's Name	**Patterns Noticed in Running Records**		
	Meaning	Structure	Visual
Max	strong	no errors	uses to self-correct
Monica	strong	walk / walks	doesn't attend to visual all the time, but substitutions make sense
Mohammed	sounds out words w/out thinking about meaning at times	omits -ed, -s endings at times	needs help w/ long & short vowels

Notes: * include Mohammed more in discussion of text to attend more to meaning; set purpose for rdg.
* pocket chart w.s. - building sentences (verb tense)
* word study w.s. - practice long/short vowels, esp. Mohammed

Figure 10.2 Student Reading Sheet

Looking at Patterns in Student Reading			
Group Red Date 10-15-02			
Child's Name	**Patterns Noticed in Student Reading**		
	Decoding	Fluency	Comprehension
Briana	some beginning sounds; knows HF words - I, like	choppy	good listening comprehension
Chrisshunda	knows many sounds; y/w confusion	getting more fluent w/ rereading	can retell story
Dior	using beginning sounds consistently; neglects ending sounds	choppy	needs work
Jasmine	over reliance on pictures - needs work on beginning sounds	choppy	good listening comprehension
Delila	knows about 1/2 of letter sounds	sounds fluent after reading (good at memorizing text)	can retell story w/ support

Notes: * need to work on beginning sounds & fluency
* do rereading of familiar text for fluency
* continue practice at Drama work station for retelling

Figure 10.3 Planning for Literacy Work Stations: Emergent Stage

If you see this:	Directly teach this:	Then have the child practice at this literacy work station:	Suggested activities at the work station:
Tries one-to-one matching	Make the words match as you point and read in shared and guided reading.	Big Book work station Poetry work station Pocket chart work station	Mark known words with highlighter tape before reading. Use pointer to one-to-one match. Read short text. Build text word by word at the pocket chart.
Just flipping pages in books	Model how to read like a beginning reader by using the pictures to tell the story in read-aloud.	Classroom library Listening work station	Tell the story aloud as you read. Read the book to a stuffed animal. Read parts you know with the tape.
Holds book upside down	Model how to hold a book in read-aloud and shared reading.	Classroom library Listening work station	"Pretend read" books. Turn pages with the tape at the listening station.
Writes some known words	Model how to use words you know in your writing with the word wall in modeled and shared writing.	ABC/word study work station Writing work station	Play games with word wall words at the ABC/word study station. Make pattern books at the writing station.
Writes some beginning sounds	Model how to use sounds you know in your name and from the ABC chart in shared and interactive writing.	Writing work station ABC/word study work station	Write daily news with a partner at the writing station. Make or sort words at the ABC/word study work station. Use the ABC and names charts at the writing station.

word incorrectly, glance at the picture, and then self-correct?

Be sure to make notes about fluency when observing children's reading. How fluent are they? Are they reading expressively? Do they have a good rate of reading, or is the reading labored? Do they read word by word?

Also note their comprehension. Have children retell what they just read or tell generally what the piece was about, then consider their level of comprehension. After reading, do they have a good grasp of what the piece was about, or do they just tell you the last detail they read?

You might use the "Looking at Patterns in Student Reading" sheet in Appendix I to record what you notice about students' decoding, fluency, and comprehension. Figure 10.2 provides an example of a completed sheet.

After you have identified what children are doing well and what they need next, you might use the Planning for Instruction at Literacy Work Stations charts in Figures 10.3–10.5. Use these to help you plan appropriate work station activities for students in the emergent, early, and transitional reading stages.

Figure 10.4 Planning for Literacy Work Stations: Early Stage

If you see this:	Directly teach this:	Then have the child practice at this literacy work station:	Suggested activities at the work station:
Uses picture and sometimes first sound of words	"Use the picture and the words to help you" in shared and guided reading. Mask some words in shared reading.	Big Book work station Buddy reading work station Classroom library Poetry work station	Read and reread familiar text. Mask some words with sticky notes before reading and then try to figure them out while reading. Find a word that matches a picture.
Not using meaning while reading; relies mostly on visual information	Mask some words in shared reading—"think what would make sense" here. Ask "What would make sense?" in guided reading.	Big Book work station Classroom library Buddy reading work station Poetry work station Listening work station	Read and reread familiar text. Mask some words with sticky notes before reading and then try to figure them out while reading. Read along with familiar books at the listening work station.
Rereads to confirm word	"You read it again and made it make sense. Keep doing that" in guided reading. Model in shared reading.	Big Book work station Buddy reading work station Classroom library Poetry work station	Read and reread familiar text. Read with a partner. Build a poem with a partner and read it again and again.
Choppy reading	Model fluent reading in read-aloud. Reread in shared reading so "it sounds like talking."	Buddy reading work station Big Book work station Classroom library Poetry work station Drama work station	Read and reread so it sounds like talking. Take parts while reading and act them out. Practice reading so you can perform for an audience.
Writes some beginning and ending sounds	"Say it and listen for sounds you know as you write" in shared and interactive writing.	ABC/word study work station Writing work station	Use ABC/name charts for sounds you hear as you work at the writing station. Write with a buddy. Make, sort, or write words at the ABC/word study work station.

Looking at Writing

Students' writing can also yield valuable information you can use in planning for instruction at literacy work stations. Observe students while they do interactive writing. Note what they find confusing, such as letter formation, what letter to use, rules of grammar, word pronunciation, and so forth.

Lay out some student writing samples across a table or the floor. (You might begin with the work of your struggling writers.) Look at the children's ideas first:

■ What do students like to write about? What do they know well?

Figure 10.5 Planning for Literacy Work Stations: Transitional Stage

If you see this:	Directly teach this:	Then have the child practice at this literacy work station:	Suggested activities at the work station:
Word calling with no attention to meaning	Set a purpose as you read in read-aloud, shared and guided reading. Give children chances to talk with a partner about what they just read.	Classroom library Big Book work station Poetry work station Buddy reading work station Buddy journals	Read and talk about what you read with a friend. Share a favorite part with a buddy. Write down something new you learned as you read today. Write in your reading log.
Easily loses interest in a longer book	Model how to choose a book; label books in tubs.	Classroom library Buddy reading work station	Read a book in a series that a friend is also reading. Use the labeled tubs in the classroom library.
Not making transition to silent reading	Model what silent reading looks and feels like. Expect silent reading.	Classroom library Listening work station	Whisper/silent reading in the classroom library. Read silently "in your head" as you listen to a tape.
Slow rate of reading; little fluency	Model fluent reading in read-aloud. Reread in shared reading so "it sounds like talking."	Buddy reading work station Big Book work station Classroom library Poetry work station Drama work station	Read and reread so it sounds like talking. Take parts while reading and act them out. Practice reading so you can perform for an audience. Use highlighter tape on punctuation and read in one breath to that mark.
Writing longer pieces with *and . . . and . . . and*	Consider audience and how interesting this sounds. Look at favorite books and number of *and*s on a page. Model writing many forms.	Classroom library Writing work station Listening work station with buddy journals	Read and reread favorite books; think about the author's craft of writing. Write books, cards, letters, and so on.

- Do they all write about the same topic, or have you given them a choice? What choices do they make?

- Do they choose one idea and stay with it?

Then, consider the kind of writing they do:

- Are they writing lists, letters, stories, reports, surveys, narratives, book reviews, summaries, comparisons, descriptions, and/or . . . ?

- What genres do students use best in writing?

- Which genres are they interested in, but could use some support with writing?

Next, look at their understanding of audience:

- Are the children aware of their audience?

- Who is their audience?

- Who else could they write to or for?

Also consider organization:

- How is their writing organized?

- Are their ideas organized, or does the piece seem disconnected?

Think about sentence fluency:

- Do students write as they speak?

- What is their sentence structure like?

- Are there errors in grammar?

Writing conventions are also important:

- Which conventions are your students using well?

- Which conventions would help make their writing clearer to their audience?

Finally, word choice:

- Do the students vary the way they begin their sentences? What about the length of their sentences?

- Do they stick with words they know how to spell or do they try using new words?

- Is their vocabulary expanding?

Figure 10.6 Student Writing Sheet

Looking at Patterns in Student Writing

Group __Green__   Date __10-20-02__

Child's Name	Ideas	Audience/ voice	Organization	Sentence fluency	Conventions	Word choice
Jordan	pets	I like ... needs sense of audience	ok	ok	spelling short vowels well	sense of audience will help this
Justin	pets	sounded just like him	good	good - work on varying sent. beginnings	mixes caps & lower-case often	
Terran	family	writes to Mom	connected	ok	get HF words under control	ok
Erick	cousin	wrote letter	jumped around a bit	choppy at times	work on short vowels	tried a few big words - xrsiz exercise

Notes:
* have good ideas - share w/ class
* help Jordan w/ audience - show him how to write letters, like T. & E. - post sample at Writing w.s.
* have Erick tell his story to group 1st & at Writing w.s.
* practice short vowels at Word Study w.s.

After you have collected information on your students' writing, use the "Looking at Patterns in Student Writing" form in Appendix I to help you make teaching decisions. Figure 10.6 shows a completed form.

Establishing a System for Collecting Data

Many teachers watch children and take mental notes but don't have a system for writing these down. With proper planning you can develop a way to take written notes on a regular basis. The thought of making written observations of all your students every day or looking at all their running records and writing samples can be overwhelming. But if you have a system of looking at several students or one or two work stations a day, the process of collecting data will be more manageable.

For example, you might begin by using the clipboard method described in the first section of this chapter to collect observational data on a different guided reading group each week. Over the course of a month or so, you will have easily collected written observations of each student in the class. At the beginning of the school year, use the clipboard assessment method daily during literacy work station time as you train children to use the work stations before you even begin to pull together small groups. A little later in the year, when your guided reading groups are up and running, observe students at least twice a month during literacy work station time. This means that you may have to forfeit one guided reading group every two weeks and take that twenty-minute block of time to walk around the work stations observing students. This activity can become a valued part of your literacy instruction routine.

Some teachers like to use a reading assessment notebook for each child, as described by Sharon Taberski in her book *On Solid Ground* (2000). You could use these notebooks to record your observations of children in reading conferences as well as in literacy work stations and during guided reading.

An assessment notebook containing notes and photos about one student's literacy behavior.

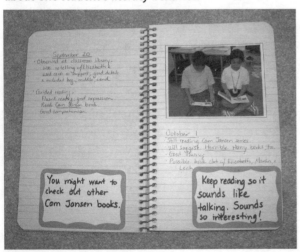

You might occasionally snap a photo of each student while he or she is working at a station and include the photo in the child's assessment notebook. Such photos can serve as visual reminders for students of what they should be doing at work stations, as well as a handy piece of information to share with parents at conferences.

Another way to collect information about your students is to plan on "eyeballing" one literacy work station each day during guided reading time. Most teachers have learned how to work with one group while constantly surveying the rest of the class to be sure that everyone is on task. Choose one station a day and "eyeball" it. You might even report to students what you noticed during literacy work station sharing time.

As you look at a work station, of course, you'll have to know what you're looking for. Use the forms that list what to look for in the various work stations at the end of Appendixes B–G to help you focus your observations at each work station. Let students know what you expect to see, too. You might use the forms as models and modify them to create your own sets of expectations for each work station. Older students (mid-first grade and second grade) can help you develop these forms.

Grades: Focus on Practice, Not Products

Literacy work stations are places for practice. Students are engaged in the process of learning to read and write and work with letters and words at the stations. By definition, if children are practicing something, we should not expect perfection. They should feel free to take risks and make approximations. Of course, over time they should gain proficiency.

Nevertheless, we live and work in an era of high accountability. I am often asked, "How can I get grades at literacy work stations? Shouldn't I have my students produce something tangible at all the stations?" My answer is, "You can take grades at some work stations, but don't try to take them *every day* at *all* of the stations. And please don't try to attach a product to every station!"

Many teachers have tried to make everything students do at literacy work stations result in some kind of tangible, gradable product. As a result, teachers often make more work for themselves than necessary. Before they know it, they have more papers to grade than they could possibly need. Worse, the drive for products begins to dictate what teachers plan for students to do at work stations. Instead, you should determine how many reading grades you really need by the end of the six- or nine-week grading period, and then plan accordingly. Many districts require only one or two grades per week in reading.

On the issue of grades, begin by asking yourself, "What do I want students to practice at literacy work stations?" From this you can find opportunities to take grades on *some* things your students practice, especially on tasks they have been practicing for a while. As you select what you want to take grades on, consider a balance of *process* and *product.*

Grades from *products* are perhaps easier to gather. Many things produced at literacy work stations can be used for grading. For example, pieces created at the writing work station can easily be graded. So can responses to books read at the classroom library or listened to at the listening work station, sentences written with spelling words at the word study work station, and names copied at the handwriting work station.

Let students know where you expect products and tell them what products you will grade. For example, if you have modeled how to write book reviews and students have had a chance to practice writing them for a while, then it is reasonable, and students may expect, that you would tell them that the book reviews they produce in the next few weeks at the literacy work stations will be graded. Post a model at the station for them to use as a benchmark.

You can also take a grade from watching the *process* of what students are practicing at literacy work stations. Begin by thinking about what you want students to practice doing, and list specific reading and writing behaviors you expect to see. If you are using one of the forms for literacy work stations from the appendixes, you can get a grade from watching what children do while at a specific work station. Think about what you value most for students to practice at that work station, and then assign points accordingly. See the sample in Figure 10.7.

Remember that literacy work stations are designed for meaningful independent practice. Plan tasks at work stations that will provide children with focused practice. Don't just plan activities with products in mind. Think about students' needs first, then plan for some products at work stations, as appropriate.

How to Document Progress for Parents

Literacy work stations provide wonderful opportunities for documenting progress to share with parents (through parent-teacher conferences and report cards). You might take photos of students while they are at work stations and include one or two in each child's report card or with progress reports. A picture is worth a thousand words! Again, you should set up a system for capturing these images. Perhaps you could simply make a list of your students' names and check off when you've taken a photo of each child at a station. You might consider doing this twice a year, once in the first half and again in the second half.

Anecdotal records written on your clipboard cards will prove very handy during parent conferences. Parents will be pleased to see how well you know their children and how carefully you've recorded observations about their work and literacy behavior. During conferences, you might also show parents some of the work their children did during

Figure 10.7 Classroom Library Assessment Form

Child's Name	Chooses a just-right book	Reads a book (not just looking at pictures)	Rereads to under-stand	Might tell the story using the pictures	Tells someone in the library about the book	Cares for materials	Literature response	Final grade
Rebecca	✓	✓	——	——	✓	✓	✓	79
Kaitlin	✓	✓	✓	✓	✓	✓	✓	90
Jessie	✓+	✓+	✓	✓	✓+	✓	✓+	96
Roberto	——	——	——	✓	✓	✓	✓-	71
Vivian	——	——	——	✓-	——	✓+	✓-	64
Zoya	✓	✓	——	——	✓	✓	✓	79

✓+ = 100	✓ = 90	✓- = 75	__ = 50

work station time. Save several samples, or ask students to save samples in their literacy work station folders, for you to show parents. You might also invite parents to visit during work station time, so they can see the kinds of things their children are practicing.

Using Work Station Sharing Time to Collect Information

During sharing time (five to ten minutes of reflection with your class following work station activities), you can learn much about your students and how they are using their practice time. By inviting students to tell what they did at the work stations,

you can hear what they actually did during this time. You can find out what's going well and (with student input) what might need to be changed. You can solve problems together. Sometimes students may bring products to share. During sharing time, children get ideas from each other about ways to behave and things to do at the work stations. (See the section on sharing time in Chapter 2, and use the sharing time questions there.)

Work Stations for the Emergent Stage of Literacy

Emergent readers' needs differ from those of students at other stages of literacy. Think about the kinds of reading and writing behavior you want students to control at this level. For example, emergent readers need to have phonological awareness, develop print awareness and concepts about print, and begin to learn about letters and sounds. They should be experimenting with writing and trying to use letters or letter-like forms to record messages. Use Figure 10.3 to help you plan for students at this level. Look at the reading and writing behaviors on the left-hand side of the chart and then plan accordingly for what each child needs to practice. Though the chart is not extensive, it can serve as a starting point for planning for individual needs at literacy work stations.

Work Stations for the Early Stage of Literacy

Children at the early stage of literacy are learning to read and write high-frequency words. They are also learning to decode and spell many single-syllable words. They use pictures and print to construct meaning, both in their reading and in their writing. They are acquiring fluency as they read and reread familiar text during work station time. Their writing is also getting more fluent, and others can easily read their messages. They reread to self-correct and attend well to print. With practice, they will become successful readers and writers.

Use Figure 10.4 to help you examine the reading and writing behaviors of students in the early stage of literacy development and to choose appropriate activities for your students to practice. Remember, this planning is just a starting point. Use your expertise to develop further tasks that meet your students' needs.

Work Stations for Transitional Readers

Transitional readers and writers have special needs, too. These children are gaining in fluency as they

learn to read and write with greater ease. However, as they move to longer texts their fluency may decrease. At this level, they often have good decoding skills, but may lack comprehension. Or they may have difficulty with decoding longer words or certain vowel patterns. They need to learn to sustain interest and attention when reading longer books and writing longer pieces. They are making the transition to silent reading and are learning to do more editing and revising. They need to expand their reading and writing to a variety of genres.

As you use Figure 10.5, think about your particular students and which activities will help them be more successful as transitional readers and writers. Again, use the form as a catalyst for your own ideas. Use the chart as a springboard for planning.

Changes in Work Stations During Second Grade

As many students in second grade move into the transitional stage of reading and writing, your work stations will have to change to reflect their needs. In kindergarten and first grade, many students are in the emergent and early stages of reading. Their work stations will involve much oral reading practice and writing of one short piece at a time.

However, by the middle of second grade average-progress students are reading silently. This will bring a new look to your literacy work stations. At this point, you might want to move to longer periods of time for students at the stations. In kindergarten and first grade, many teachers have each rotation last about fifteen minutes. In mid-second grade you will want to lengthen the amount of time children spend at some stations to twenty or possibly twenty-five minutes to encourage them to extend their reading and writing stamina. Students should be helped to read and write about topics of interest for longer periods of time. At this stage, they may go to only two longer work stations instead of three shorter ones.

Independent reading takes up a bigger portion of independent work time for children at this stage. They often read and then write responses to what they read, sometimes in preparation for literature discussion groups or literature circles. They still enjoy using the computer, but may be using it more for research and/or publishing their writing. You might keep some shorter-duration work stations open, such as the overhead or the listening station, for these students to use. But the general move should be toward more sustained independent practice. Some teachers continue to use a management board, but they indicate the shorter and longer work stations on it by color-coding the icons. For example, longer-lasting stations might be red and shorter ones yellow.

You might begin work station time for these students with quiet work, where all are to be seated at their desks doing silent reading and writing responses for the first twenty-five to thirty minutes. Then use the remaining time for more active pursuits, with students moving to a variety of work stations around the classroom, such as the drama, poetry, overhead, word study, and buddy reading stations.

In second grade, beware of the temptation to make all your work stations product-oriented. Again, the process of practicing reading and writing should be valued, and these practice sessions can be assessed. It is still important to observe students' reading and writing behavior at this stage, but you will probably learn more by conferring with and talking to children about their work, as much of it is now being done silently.

Work Stations for Second Language Learners

As you consider the needs of all your students, be aware of your second language learners. Although they may be reading on grade level in their native language, they often need additional opportunities for oral language development in English. Try to pair your second language learners with more fluent English speakers at the work stations to help them develop their English oral language skills. Here are a few ideas on how to integrate more oral language into some of your work stations for them.

Listening work station: Second language learners will benefit from additional models of spoken English, which they can easily get from listening to books on tape. Listening to favorite books over and over again is especially effective. Books that have been read aloud, acted out, and discussed in class are even more helpful. After students listen to a book on tape, have them sit knee to knee and talk with each other about it.

Classroom library: Place books that have been read aloud and discussed into the classroom library for students to read and reread. Second language learners should be encouraged to tell the story using the pictures. This will help them develop a sense of story as well as practice with the language. Keeping the emphasis on oral language for a period of time will help develop fluency.

Big Book work station: Opportunities to participate in the reading of books in shared reading will offer support for the second language learner. At the Big Book work station, a child can practice reading the book with the support of a partner who reads and speaks English fluently. After reading together, the two can talk about the book, discussing the characters, new information they have learned, and their favorite parts, or asking each other questions about the book.

Drama work station: The drama station is one of the best work stations for developing oral language. After repeated readings of read-aloud books that have several main characters, the story can be retold, with the characters represented by puppets or illustrated on a felt board. Second language learners can help retell the story with a partner using these props.

Writing work station: Encourage second language learners to tell their partners what they're planning to write about at the writing work station. Have the partners listen and tell what they understood their partners to say. Have the pairs work together to tell the "story" first; then let them write it together.

Word study work station: Have available objects and/or pictures to sort and to use as a springboard for discussion at the word study work station. Many second language learners need to improve their phonemic awareness of English sounds. Picture sorts are invaluable here. Pictures and objects can also be used for naming and for sentence development.

Buddy reading work station: At the buddy reading station, the fluent English speaker might read the book to the second language learner. The child learning English might then retell the book or ask his or her partner questions about the book.

Poetry work station: Poetry can be used to help students learn English. The English-speaking reader might read a poem to his or her partner, who listens for rhyming words or words beginning with certain sounds. Or students might chorally reread familiar poems taught during shared reading. Then they can look for rhyming words or words that begin or end with particular sounds. This can help a child learn the sounds and rhythms of English.

Reflection and Dialogue

Consider the following:

1. Make a clipboard assessment tool with a friend. Challenge each other to use this to gather anecdotal notes on at least several stu-

dents during the next week or two. You might each choose to observe a low-, a medium-, and a high-performing student in your respective classrooms. Then plan a time to get together again in two weeks and share your notes. Use your observations to plan some work station activities for those particular students.

2. Choose one work station. Observe students there and look for differentiation. Are the needs of each child being met? Which tasks are multi-level? Which are open-ended? What can you change or add to better meet the needs of all students in your classroom at this work station? Share your findings and ideas with a colleague.

3. Gather running records for one of your guided reading groups. You might take a low or a high group to begin (since most teachers tend to teach to the middle). Examine the running records for patterns, using the "Looking at Patterns in Running Records" form. Do this with another teacher and compare notes. Then use the information gleaned to plan for practice at literacy work stations for this group.

4. Likewise, look at a set of writing samples for a group of students. You might use the same group as in the example above. Examine the pieces for patterns and make notes. Then use that information to plan for practice at literacy work stations. You will probably think of activities for the word study and writing work stations. But you might also consider the listening station if you want to expose students to higher vocabulary or extra models of reading fluency and English language usage.

5. Create a system for collecting data on what students are doing at the literacy work stations. You might use the clipboard assessment method or another way of gathering data, such as eyeballing one work station a day. Share your system with a colleague and compare how it's going over time.

6. Share with another teacher how you are getting grades during literacy work station time. Support each other by sharing ideas of how to balance grades taken from your observations of students' processes and products.

7. Talk with other teachers and your administrators about how you're sharing with parents what students do at the literacy work stations.

Show photos taken, anecdotal notes recorded, and products saved. Be proactive!

8. Take notes during work station sharing time and talk about them with a colleague. What did you learn from your dialogue with the children? What changes did you (or will you) make as a result of these conversations?

Appendix

A

Icons for Work Stations

My Literacy
Work Station Folder

Mi carpeta de estacion
de trabajo literario

Classroom Library

Biblioteca del salón

Big Book Work Station

Estación de trabajo de superlibros

Writing Work Station

Estación de trabajo de escritura

Drama Work Station

Estación de trabajo de dramatización

ABC/Word Study Work Station

Estación de trabajo de estudio del alfabeto y palabras

Poetry Work Station

Estación de trabajo de poesía

Rain on the rooftop.
Rain on the tree.
Rain on the green grass.
But not on me.

Literacy Work Stations: Making Centers Work by Debbie Diller. Copyright © 2003. Stenhouse Publishers.

Computer Work Station

Estación de trabajo de computadoras

Listening Work Station

Estación de trabajo de escuchar

Puzzles and Games
Work Station

Estación de trabajo de
rompecabezas y juegos

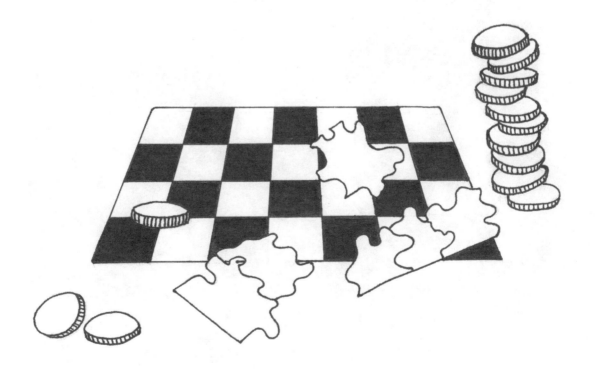

Buddy Reading Work Station

Estación de trabajo de leer con un compañero

Overhead Work Station

Estación de trabajo del proyector de transparencias

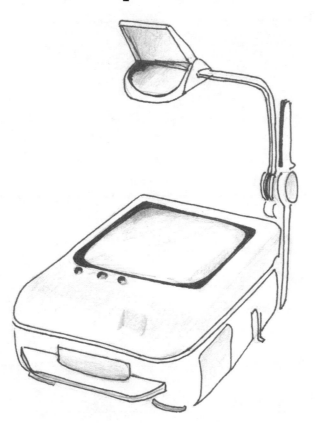

Pocket Chart
Work Station

Estación de trabajo de
carta de bolsillos

Twinkle, twinkle, little star,

How I wonder what you are.

Up above the world so high,

Like a diamond in the sky.

Literacy Work Stations: Making Centers Work by Debbie Diller. Copyright © 2003. Stenhouse Publishers.

Creation Work Station

Estación de trabajo de creación

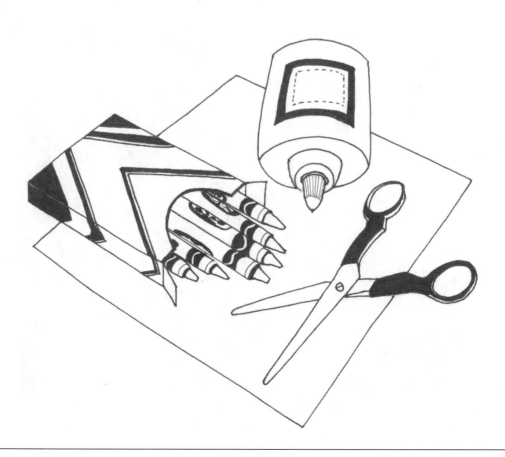

Science Work Station

Estación de trabajo de ciencias

Social Studies Work Station

Estación de trabajo de estudios sociales

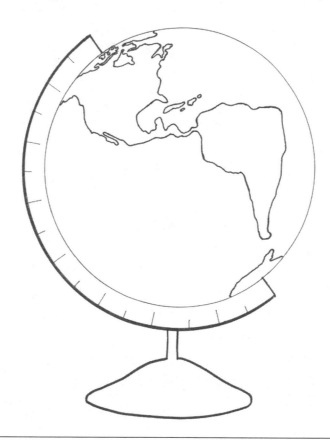

Handwriting Work Station

Estación de trabajo de letra escrita

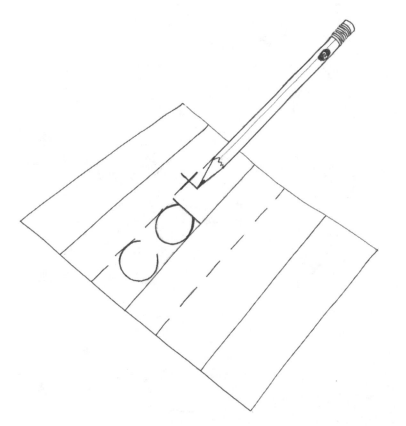

Housekeeping
Work Station

Estación de trabajo de
quehacer

Blocks Work Station

Estación de trabajo de bloques

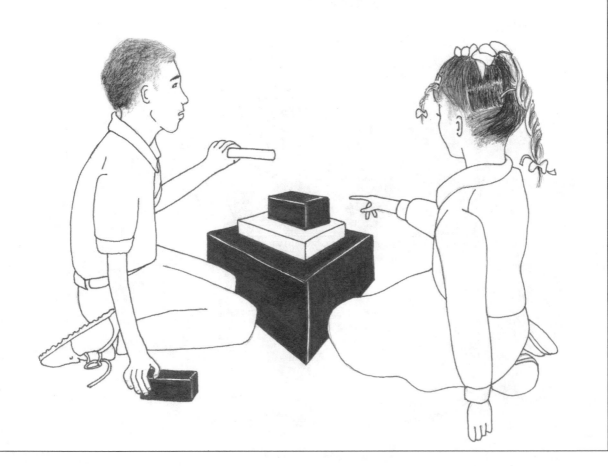

Literacy Work Stations: Making Centers Work by Debbie Diller. Copyright © 2003. Stenhouse Publishers.

Sand or Water Work Station

Estación de trabajo de arena y agua

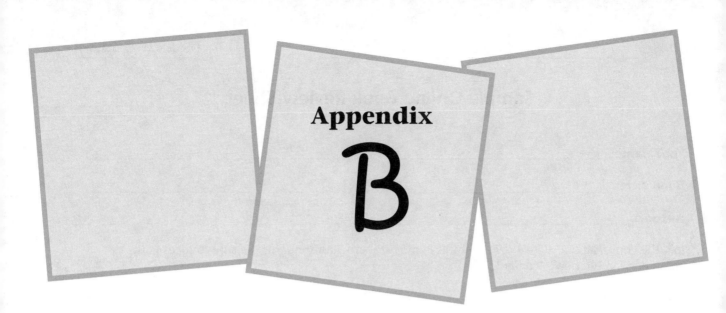

Appendix

B

Resources for the Classroom Library

Sample Online Book Review Sheet

Your name: _____

Book title: _____

Author: _____

Join the conversation! Write a review of this item and share your thoughts. Be sure to focus your comments on the book's content.

Let's get started!

On a scale of 1 to 5 stars, with 5 being the best,

1.   How do you rate this book?

     ☆   ☆   ☆   ☆   ☆

2.   Enter a title for your review.

     ┌───┐
     │   │
     │   │
     └───┘

3.   Write your review in the space below.

     ┌───┐
     │   │
     │   │
     │   │
     │   │
     │   │
     │   │
     └───┘

4.   Where in the world are you? (Example: Houston, Texas, USA)

     ┌───┐
     │   │
     │   │
     └───┘

5.   How old are you?

     ┌───┐
     │   │
     │   │
     └───┘

Muestra de la forma de crítica de libros

Tu nombre: _____

Título del libro: _____

Autor: _____

¡Conversa con nosotros! Escribe una crítica de este libro y comparte tus pensamientos con nosotros.

¡Empecemos!

En una escala de 1 a 5 estrellas, 5 siendo lo mejor,

1. ¿Cómo calificas este libro?

    ☆   ☆   ☆   ☆   ☆

2. Dale un título a tu crítica.

3. Escribe tu crítica en el espacio de abajo.

4. ¿En qué lugar del mundo vives? (Ejemplo: Houston, Texas, USA)

5. ¿Cuántos años tienes?

Goal-Setting Sheet

My Reading Goals

Name: _____ **Date:** _____

This week I read

```
┌─────────────────────────────────────────────────────────────┐
│                                                             │
│                                                             │
│                                                             │
│                                                             │
│                                                             │
└─────────────────────────────────────────────────────────────┘
```

Next week I plan to read

```
┌─────────────────────────────────────────────────────────────┐
│                                                             │
│                                                             │
│                                                             │
│                                                             │
│                                                             │
└─────────────────────────────────────────────────────────────┘
```

Something I did well in reading this week was

```
┌─────────────────────────────────────────────────────────────┐
│                                                             │
│                                                             │
│                                                             │
│                                                             │
└─────────────────────────────────────────────────────────────┘
```

Next week in reading I want to get better at

```
┌─────────────────────────────────────────────────────────────┐
│                                                             │
│                                                             │
│                                                             │
│                                                             │
└─────────────────────────────────────────────────────────────┘
```

Hoja con mis metas

Mis metas de lectura

Nombre: _____ **Fecha:** _____

Esta semana leí

La próxima semana pienso leer

Algo que hice bien al leer esta semana fué

La próxima semana quiero mejorar lo siguiente al leer

Sample Reading Log

My Weekly Reading Log

Name: _____ **Week of:** _____

Monday

Title: _____

Author: _____

Tuesday

Title: _____

Author: _____

Wednesday

Title: _____

Author: _____

Thursday

Title: _____

Author: _____

Friday

Title: _____

Author: _____

In the square, mark the kind of reading you did: **F = fiction**   **NF = nonfiction**   **P = poetry**
In the circle, draw a face and show how your reading went today.

Literacy Work Stations: Making Centers Work by Debbie Diller. Copyright © 2003. Stenhouse Publishers.

Muestra de récord de lectura

Mis metas de lectura

Nombre: _____ **Semana de:** _____

lunes

Título: _____

Autor: _____

martes

Título: _____

Autor: _____

miércoles

Título: _____

Autor: _____

jueves

Título: _____

Autor: _____

viernes

Título: _____

Autor: _____

En el cuadro, marca el tipo de libro que leíste: **F = ficción**   **NF = no ficción**   **P = poesía**
En el círculo, dibuja una cara para enseñar como fuiste hoy en tu lectura.

Reading Response Sheet: Book Talk

Book Talk

Your name: _____ **Date:** _____

Book title: _____

Author: _____

Draw your face to show how you liked this book.

Write what you thought about the book in the speech bubble.

Hojas de repuesta a la lectura: Hablar de los libros

Hablar de los libros

Tu nombre: _____ **Fecha:** _____

Título del libro: _____

Autor: _____

Dibuja la expression de tu cara cuando estabas leyendo este libro.

Escribe lo que pensaste del libro que leíste en el cuadro proveído.

Reading Response Sheet: Happy Face Book Review

Happy Face Book Review

Your name: _____ **Date:** _____

Book title: _____

Author: _____

Color in the number of happy faces to show how much you liked the book.

1. ☺ = not very much

5. ☺ = a whole lot

Draw and write about your favorite part of the book.

☺   ☺   ☺   ☺   ☺

_____

_____

_____

_____

_____

Hoja de respuesta a lectura: Revisión de libros "Carita felíz"

Revisión de libros "Carita felíz"

Tu nombre: _____ **Fecha:** _____

Título del libro: _____

Autor: _____

Colorea el número de "Caritas felices" para mostrar cúanto te gustó el libro.

1. ☺ = no mucho

5. ☺ = muchísimo

Dibuja y escribe acerca de tu parte favorita del libro.

☺   ☺   ☺   ☺   ☺

_____

_____

_____

_____

_____

Reading Response Sheet: Tell a Friend

Tell a Friend

Your name: _____ **Date:** _____

Book title: _____

Author: _____

In this book, I liked

In this book, I didn't like

Who do you think would like this book? Why?

Literacy Work Stations: Making Centers Work by Debbie Diller. Copyright © 2003. Stenhouse Publishers.

Hoja de respuesta a la lectura: Cuéntale a un amigo

Cuéntale a un amigo

Tu nombre: _____ **Fecha:** _____

Título del libro: _____

Autor: _____

Lo que me gustó de este libro fué

Lo que no me gustó de este libro fué

¿A quién crees que le gustaría este libro? ¿Porqué?

Reading Response Sheet: My Book About a Book I Read

My Book About a Book I Read

Write the title and author of the book on page 1. Draw and write on the other pages. Cut and make your own book about the book you read. Put it in the classroom library for others to read.

My Book About	The part I liked best was
_____	
(title of book you read)	
_____	
(author of book you read)	
by	
_____	
(your name)	
Page 1	Page 2
This book reminded me of	This book made me feel
	because
Page 3	Page 4

Literacy Work Stations: Making Centers Work by Debbie Diller. Copyright © 2003. Stenhouse Publishers.

Hoja de respuesta a la lectura: Mi libro acerca de un libro que leí

Mi libro acerca de un libro que leí

Escribe el título y autor del libro en la página 1. Dibuja y escribe en las otras páginas. Recorta y has tu propio libro acerca del libro que leíste. Pónlo en la biblioteca del salón para que otros puedan leerlo.

Mi libro acerca de _____ (título del libro que leíste) _____ (autor del libro que leíste) por _____ (tu nombre) Página 1	La parte que más me gusto fué Página 2
Este libro me recordó de Página 3	Este libro me hizo sentir porque Página 4

Checklist for Your Classroom Library

Goals for This Work Station:

- Work with familiar text to develop concepts about print.
- Develop love of books and reading.
- Read or "pretend read."
- Talk about books read.
- Write about books read.
- Classify and learn about a variety of literary genres.

Date	Materials to Be Added or Changed
	"Classroom Library" sign
	Bookshelves labeled "fiction" and "nonfiction"
	Open-faced book rack for displaying books with covers showing
	Wide variety of books, including fiction and nonfiction
	Other print materials, such as magazines, newspapers, menus, etc.
	Books representing cultures of all students in your classroom (and beyond)
	Containers to hold books, sorted by genre, author, level, etc., and labeled by the children
	Student-made books
	Comfortable seating (beanbag chairs, futon, large pillows)
	Silk plant or flowers in a pot (something alive or that looks like it's alive)
	Lamp
	Rug to define the space
	Tape recorder playing soft music
	Stuffed animals for children to read to
	Book reviews/responses written by the class and by individual students
	Author study materials, including information about an author posted and a tub of books by that author in a labeled container
	Bookmarks
	"How to Choose a Book" chart made by the class
	"How to Write a Book Review" chart made by the class
	Clipboards with book response forms and pencil attached
	Sticky notes
	"Our Favorite Books" album

Literacy Work Stations: Making Centers Work by Debbie Diller. Copyright © 2003. Stenhouse Publishers.

Classroom Library Assessment Form

Teacher Name: _____   Date: _____

Child's name	Chooses a just-right book	Reads a book (not just looking at pictures)	Rereads to understand	Might tell the story using the pictures	Tells some-one in the library about the book	Cares for materials	Literature response

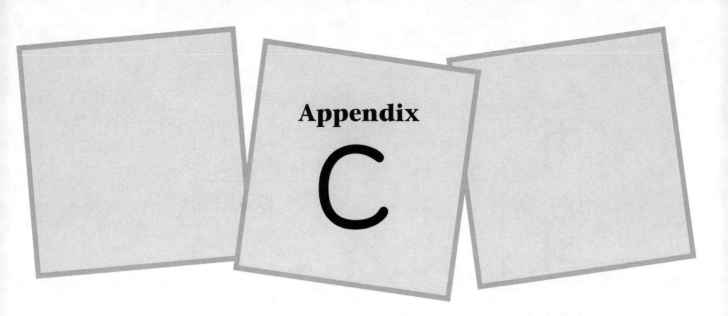

Appendix
C

Resources for the
Big Book Work Station

Big Books Work Station Assessment Form: Emergent/Early Reader

Teacher Name: _____   Date: _____

Child's name	One-to-one matching	Left to right; top to bottom	Finds known words	Turns pages carefully	Reads with fluency and expression	Retells book/ dramatizes

Big Book Task Cards

A word you know you know	Two words that rhyme
the	*cat* *hat*
A word that ends in a vowel	A word that has 2 syllables
one	**look***ing*

Spanish Big Book Task Cards

Una palabra que conoces *el*	Una palabra que tiene dos vocales juntos *tia*
Una palabra que termina con un vocal ***mí***	Una palabra con dos sílabas ***ro****jo*

Big Books Work Station Assessment Form: Transitional/Fluent Reader

Teacher Name: _____

Date: _____

Child's name	Reads in phrases	Stops at punctuation	Good fluency and expression	Writes connections	Finds special words	Retells book/ dramatizes

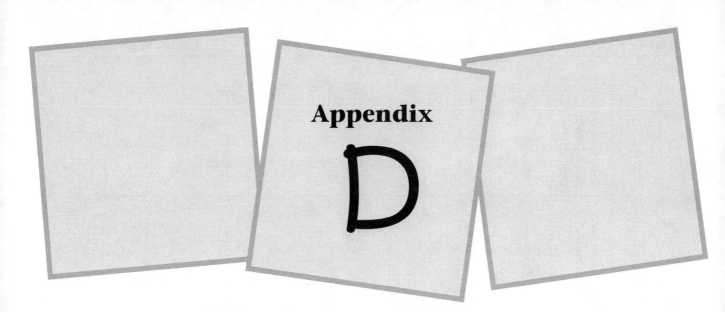

Appendix

D

Resources for the Writing Work Station

Writing Work Station Assessment Form

Teacher Name: _____ Date: _____

Child's name	Writing tool in hand	Has paper/ something to write on	Writes something	Rereads and rereads his/her writing	Shares writing (with buddy)	Uses writing helps (word wall, charts, . . .)

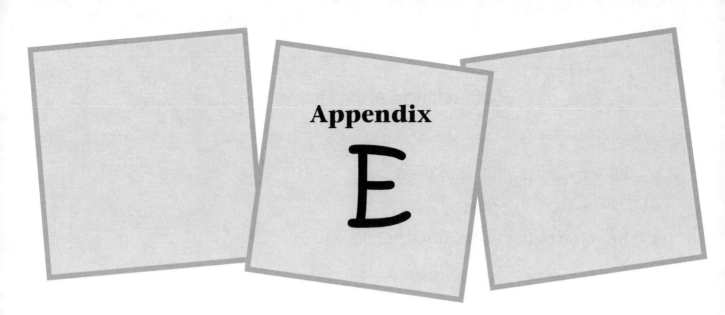

Appendix

E

Resources for the
Drama Work Station

Retelling Cards: Fiction

- Tell someone about your book.
- Tell the story in order.
- Use some of the words from the book.

Beginning

- Characters
- Setting
- How did it begin?

Middle

- What happened?
- Tell the details.
- Was there a problem? How was it solved?

End

- How did it end?
- What would you like to read next? Why?
- I think the author wrote this to _____.

Tarjetas para recontar: Ficción

- Cuéntale a alguien sobre tu libro.
- Cuénta la historia en orden.
- Usa algunas palabras del libro.

Comienzo

- Personajes
- Escena
- ¿Cómo empezó?

Medio

- ¿Qué pasó?
- Cuenta los detalles.
- ¿Hubo un problema? ¿Cómo se resolvió?

Final

- ¿Cómo terminó?
- ¿Qué te gustaría leer ahora? ¿Porqué?
- Creo que el autor escribió esto para _____.

Retelling Cards: Nonfiction

- Tell someone about your book.
- Tell what you learned in order.
- Use some of the words from the book.

Topic

- This was mostly about _____.
- It reminded me of _____.
- I noticed _____.

What I Learned

- Some things I learned are _____.
- Some new words I learned are _____.
- How did the visuals help you?
- The book also told me _____.

End

- Some questions I still have are _____.
- What would you like to read next? Why?
- I think the author wrote this to _____.

Tarjetas para recontar: No ficción

- Cuéntale a alguien sobre tu libro.
- Cuenta lo que has aprendido en orden.
- Usa algunas palabras del libro.

Tema
- Se trató de _____.
- Me recordó de _____.
- Me dí cuenta que _____.

Lo que aprendí
- Algunas cosas que aprendí _____.
- Algunas palabras nuevas que aprendí son _____.
- ¿Cómo te ayudaron las fotos?
- El libro tambien me enseñó _____.

Final
- Algunas preguntas que todavía tengo son _____.
- ¿Qué te gustaría leer ahora? ¿Porqué?
- Creo que el autor escribió esto para _____.

Sources of Easy-to-Read Plays and Reader's Theater

Internet Sources for Reader's Theater

www.readinglady.com
http://raven.jmu.edu/~ramseyil/billygoat.htm
http://raven.jmu.edu/~ramseyil/redhen.htm
www.aaronshep.com/rt/RTE.html
www.stemnet.nf.ca/CITE/langrt.htm
http://falcon.jmu.edu/~ramseyil/readersmine.htm

Sources for Short, Easy-to-Read Plays

Bany-Winters, Lisa. 1997. *On Stage: Theater Games and Activities for Kids.* Chicago: Chicago Review Press.

———. 2000. *Show Time: Music, Dance, and Drama Activities for Kids.* Chicago: Chicago Review Press.

Barchers, Suzanne. 1993. *Reader's Theater for Beginning Readers.* Greenwood Village, CO: Teacher Ideas Press.

Blau, Lisa. 1997a. *Fall Is Fabulous! Reader's Theatre Scripts and Extended Activities.* Bellevue, WA: One from the Heart.

———. 1997b. *Favorite Folktales and Fabulous Fables: Multicultural Plays with Extended Activities.* Bellevue, WA: One from the Heart.

———. 1997c. *Super Science! Readers Theatre Scripts and Extended Activities.* Bellevue, WA: One from the Heart.

Crawford, Sheryl Ann, and Nancy I. Sanders. 1999. *Fifteen Irresistible Mini-Plays for Teaching Math.* New York: Scholastic Professional Books.

———. 2001a. *Fifteen Easy-to-Read Holiday and Seasonal Mini-Book Plays.* New York: Scholastic.

———. 2001b. *Fifteen Easy-to-Read Mini-Book Plays.* New York: Scholastic.

———. 2001c. *Just Right Plays: Twenty-Five Science Plays for Emergent Readers.* New York: Scholastic Professional Books.

———. 2003. *Fifteen Easy-to-Read Neighborhood and Community Mini-Book Plays.* New York: Scholastic.

Cullum, Albert, and Janet Skiles. 1993. *Aesop's Fables: Plays for Young Children.* Parsippany, NJ: Fearon Teacher Aids.

Laughlin, Mildred, et al. 1991. *Social Studies Readers Theater for Children: Scripts and Script Development.* Englewood, CO: Libraries Unlimited.

Martin, Justin McCory. 2002. *Twelve Fabulously Funny Fairy Tale Plays.* New York: Scholastic Professional Books.

Pugliano-Martin, Carol. 1998. *Just-Right Plays: Twenty-Five Science Plays for Emergent Readers.* New York: Scholastic Professional Books.

———. 1999a. *Twenty-Five Emergent Reader Plays Around the Year.* New York: Scholastic Professional Books.

———. 1999b. *Twenty-Five Just-Right Plays for Emergent Readers.* New York: Scholastic Professional Books.

———. 1999c. *Twenty-Five Spanish Plays for Emergent Readers.* New York: Scholastic Professional Books.

———. 2002. *Fifteen Plays About Famous Americans for Emergent Readers.* New York: Scholastic Professional Books.

Pugliano, Carol, and Carolyn Croll. 1999. *Easy-to-Read Folk and Fairy Plays.* New York: Scholastic Professional Books.

Schafer, Liza, and Nancy I. Shafer. 1999. *Fifteen Easy-to-Read Mini-Book Plays.* New York: Scholastic Professional Books.

West, Tracy. 2000. *Big Book of Thematic Plays.* New York: Scholastic Professional Books.

Drama Work Station Assessment Form

Teacher Name: _____   Date: _____

Child's name	Uses a book to retell a story	Uses retelling pieces/puppets to retell	Includes beginning, middle, end in retelling	Includes details in retelling	Reads scripts	Reads/retells with fluency/expression

Resources for the
ABC/Word Study Work Station

Word Hunt Sheet: K–First Grade

Name: _____

Caza de palabras: K–Primer año

Nombre: _____

Word Hunt Sheet: Second Grade

Name: _____

Caza de palabras: Segundo año

Nombre: _____

Letter Sort Cards

Use with magnetic or foam letters.

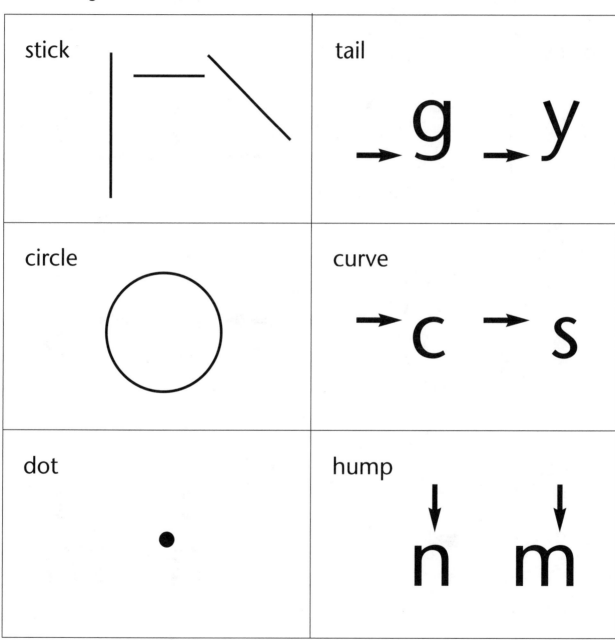

Tarjetas de letras para clasificar

Usa con letras magnéticas o de nieve seca.

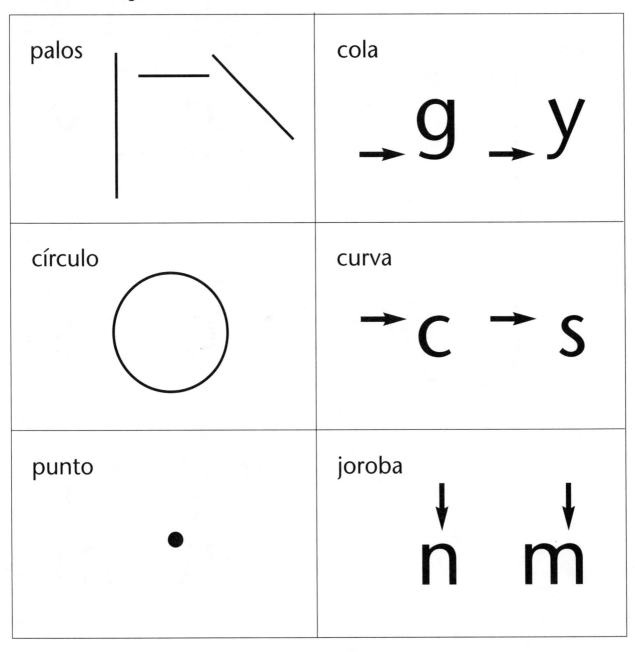

palos

cola

círculo

curva

punto

joroba

Letter Sort Cards

Use with magnetic or foam letters.

circle and stick	all sticks
◯ │	│ │ —
slant	**tall letters**
/ \	b h
below the line	**short letters**
j p	a w

Tarjetas de letras para clasificar

Usa con letras magnéticas o de nieve seca.

círculo y palo	todos palos
alsesgo	letras altas b h
abajo de la línea j p	letras bajas a w

ABC/Word Study Work Station Assessment Form: Letter Work

Teacher Name: _____   Date: _____

Child's name	Sorts letters	Names letters	Matches letters/sounds	Forms letters correctly	Puts letters in ABC order	Does ABC puzzles

ABC/Word Study Work Station Assessment Form: Word Work

Teacher Name: _____   Date: _____

Child's name	Sorts words	Reads words	Makes words	Spells words correctly	Puts words in ABC order	Plays word games

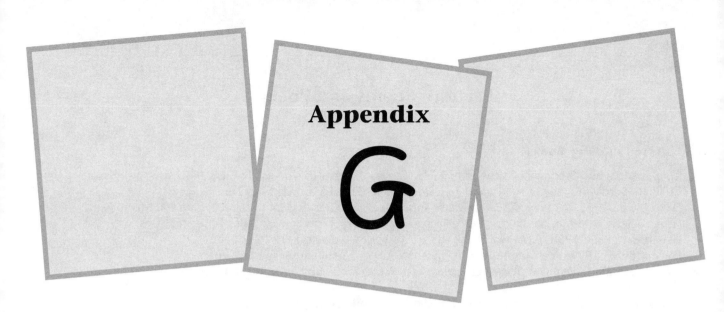

G

Resources for the Poetry Work Station

Favorite Poems and Poets

Children's Poetry Books

Cole, Joanna, and Stephanie Calmenson. 1993. *Six Sick Sheep: 101 Tongue Twisters.* New York: Scholastic.

Cullinan, Bernice E., ed. 1996. *A Jar of Tiny Stars.* Honesdale, PA: Boyds Mills Press.

Dakos, Kalli. 1992. *If You're Not Here, Please Raise Your Hand: Poems About School.* New York: Macmillan.

Fisher, Aileen. 1965. *In the Woods, In the Meadow, In the Sky.* New York: Charles Scribner's Sons.

Fleischman, Paul. 1988. *Joyful Noise: Poems for Two Voices.* New York: HarperCollins.

Franco, Betsy. 1999. *Poem of the Week* (series). San Diego: Teaching Resource Center.

———. 2002. *My Very Own Poetry Collection: 101 Poems for Kindergartners.* San Diego: Teaching Resource Center.

Hopkins, Lee Bennett, ed. 1991. *Happy Birthday.* New York: Simon & Schuster.

———. 1992a. *Flit, Flutter, Fly.* New York: Doubleday.

———. 1992b. *Through Our Eyes: Poems and Pictures About Growing Up.* Boston: Little, Brown.

———. 1996. *Opening Days: Sports Poems.* New York: Harcourt Brace & Company.

———. 1998. *Climb into My Lap: First Poems to Read Together.* New York: Simon & Schuster.

Merriam, Eve. 1988. *You Be Good and I'll Be Night.* New York: William Morrow & Company.

Prelutsky, Jack, ed.1983. *The Random House Book of Poetry.* New York: Random House.

Reiner, Marian, comp. 1999. *Month by Month Poetry* (series). New York: Scholastic.

Strickland, Dorothy S., and Michael R. Strickland, eds. 1994. *Families: Poems Celebrating the African American Experience.* Honesdale, PA: Boyds Mills Press.

Worth, Valerie. 1994. *All the Small Poems and Fourteen More.* New York: Farrar, Straus and Giroux.

Children's Poets to Study

For kindergarten:
- Arnold Adoff
- Karla Kuskin
- Dr. Seuss

For first grade:
- Aileen Fisher
- Myra Cohn Livingston
- David McCord
- Eve Merriam
- Lilian Moore
- Valerie Worth

For second grade:
- John Ciardi
- Lee Bennett Hopkins
- Langston Hughes
- Jack Prelutsky
- Christina Rosetti
- Shel Silverstein

Paired Poems

A Rocket in My Pocket
I've got a rocket
In my pocket;
I cannot stop to play.
Away it goes! I've burned my toes.
It's Independence Day.

I Love You
I love you, I love you,
I love you divine,
Please give me your bubble gum,
You're *sitting* on mine!

Toot! Toot!
A peanut sat on a railroad track,
His heart was all a-flutter;
The five-fifteen came rushing by—
Toot! Toot! peanut butter!

I've Got a Dog
I've got a dog as thin as a rail,
He's got fleas all over his tail;
Every time his tail goes flop,
The fleas on the bottom all hop to the top.

Question
Do you love me
Or do you not?
You told me once
But I forgot.

Way Down South
Way down South where bananas grow,
A grasshopper stepped on an elephant's toe.
The elephant said, with tears in his eyes,
"Pick on somebody your own size."

Poetry Work Station Assessment Form: Emergent/Early Reader

Teacher Name: _____

Date: _____

Child's name	One-to-one matches	Left to right; top to bottom	Finds known words	Reads with fluency and expression	Acts out poem	Matches word to poem

Poetry Work Station Assessment Form: Transitional/Fluent Reader

Teacher Name: _____ Date: _____

Child's name	Reads poems fluently and with good expression	Buddy reads/ discusses poems	Finds known/ special words	Manipulates words in poems	Copies and/or illustrates poems	Writes poems

Appendix

H

Resources for Other Work Stations

For the Computer Work Station

Materials Manager	Materiales encargado
Computer Expert 	Experto de computadora 

Things to Use on the Overhead

Cosas para usar en el proyector

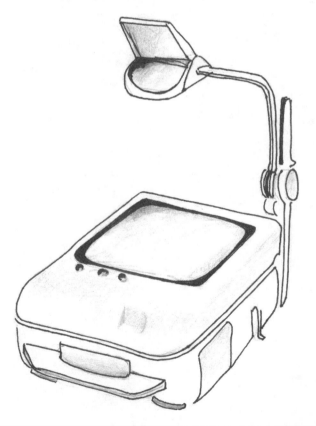

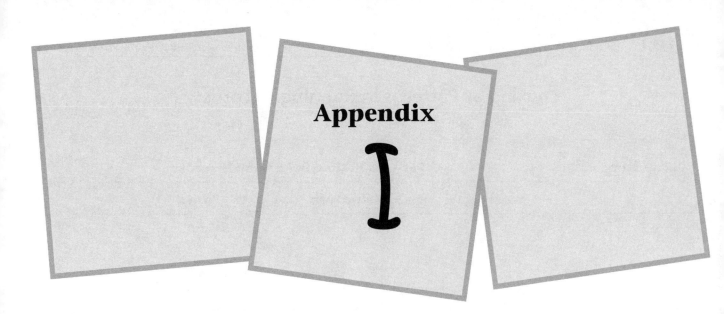

Appendix

I

Resources for Planning and Assessment

Looking at Patterns in Running Records

Group _____ Date _____

Child's Name | **Patterns Noticed in Running Records**

	Meaning	Structure	Visual

Notes:

Looking at Patterns in Student Reading

Group _____   Date _____

Child's Name	Patterns Noticed in Student Reading		
	Decoding	**Fluency**	**Comprehension**

Notes:

Looking at Patterns in Student Writing

Group _____ Date _____

Child's Name	Patterns Noticed in Student Writing					
	Ideas	Audience/ voice	Organization	Sentence fluency	Conventions	Word choice

Notes:

References

Professional Sources

Bear, D., et al. 2000. *Words Their Way: Word Study for Phonics, Vocabulary, and Spelling Instruction.* Columbus, OH: Prentice Hall.

Brown, S. 2000. *All Sorts of Sorts.* San Diego: Teaching Resource Center.

Cambourne, B. 1988. *The Whole Story: Natural Learning and the Acquisition of Literacy.* Auckland, NZ: Ashton-Scholastic.

Clay, M. 2000. *Running Records for Classroom Teachers.* Portsmouth, NH: Heinemann.

Cunningham, P. 1994. *Making Words.* Carthage, IL: Good Apple Books.

———. 1995. *Phonics They Use: Words for Reading and Writing.* Boston: Allyn and Bacon.

Diller, D. 2002. *Beyond the Names Chart: Using Children's Names for Word Study.* San Diego: Teaching Resource Center.

———. 2003. *Literacy Work Stations Task Cards.* San Diego: Teaching Resource Center.

Dorn, L. 2002. *Literacy Task Cards.* San Diego: Teaching Resource Center.

Dorn, L., and C. Soffos. 2002. *Shaping Literate Minds.* Portland, ME: Stenhouse.

Fisher, B., and E. F. Medvic. 2000. *Perspectives on Shared Reading.* Portsmouth, NH: Heinemann.

Fletcher, R., and J. Portalupi. 2001. *Writing Workshop: The Essential Guide.* Portsmouth, NH: Heinemann.

Fountas, I., and G. S. Pinnell. 1996. *Guided Reading: Good First Teaching for All Children.* Portsmouth, NH: Heinemann.

———. 1999. *Matching Books to Readers: Using Leveled Books in Guided Reading, K–3.* Portsmouth, NH: Heinemann.

Franco, B. 1998. *Poem of the Week* series. Book 1. San Diego: Teaching Resource Center.

———. 1999. *Poem of the Week* series. Book 2. San Diego: Teaching Resource Center.

———. 2002. *My Very Own Poetry Collection: 101 Poems for Kindergartners.* San Diego: Teaching Resource Center.

Freeman, M. 1998. *Teaching the Youngest Writers: A Practical Guide.* Gainesville, FL: Maupin House.

Gardner, H. 1993. *Frames of Mind: The Theory of Multiple Intelligence.* New York: Basic Books.

Harvey, S., and A. Goudvis. 2000. *Strategies That Work: Teaching Comprehension to Enhance Understanding.* Portland, ME: Stenhouse.

Holley, C. 1995. *Warming Up to Big Books.* Bothell, WA: Wright Group.

Jensen, E. 1998. *Teaching with the Brain in Mind.* Alexandria, VA: Association for Supervision and Curriculum Development.

Johnson, C. L. 1998. *Think Big! Creating Big Books with Children*. Bothell, WA: Wright Group.

Keene, E., and S. Zimmermann. 1997. *Mosaic of Thought: Teaching Comprehension in a Reader's Workshop*. Portsmouth, NH: Heinemann.

Miller, D. 2002. *Reading with Meaning: Teaching Comprehension in the Primary Grades*. Portland, ME: Stenhouse.

Parkes, B. 2000. *Read It Again! Revisiting Shared Reading*. Portland, ME: Stenhouse.

Pearson, P. D., and M. C. Gallagher. 1983. "The Instruction of Reading Comprehension." *Contemporary Educational Psychology* 8: 317–344.

Routman, R. 2000. *Kids' Poems*. New York: Scholastic.

Taberski, S. 2000. *On Solid Ground: Strategies for Teaching Reading*. Portsmouth, NH: Heinemann.

Vygotsky, L. S. 1978. *Mind in Society: The Development of Higher Psychological Processes*. Cambridge, MA: Harvard University Press.

Wagstaff, J. 1999. *Teaching Reading and Writing with Word Walls*. New York: Scholastic.

Children's Books

Bayer, J. 1984. *A, My Name Is Alice*. New York: Dial Books.

Berger, M. 1986. *Germs Make Me Sick*. New York: HarperCollins.

———. 1998. *Chirping Crickets*. New York: HarperCollins.

Cole, J. 1986. *Hungry, Hungry Sharks*. New York: Random House.

———. 1989. *The Magic School Bus: Inside the Human Body*. New York: Random House.

Cowley, J. 1989. *The Birthday Cake*. Bothell, WA: Wright Group.

———. 1995a. *Cats, Cats, Cats*. Bothell, WA: Wright Group.

———. 1995b. *The Farm Concert*. Bothell, WA: Wright Group.

Ehlert, L. 1996a. *Color Zoo*. New York: Harper Collins.

———. 1996b. *Under My Nose*. Katonah, NY: Richard C. Owen.

Neitzel, S. 1995. *The Bag I'm Taking to Grandma's*. New York: Greenwillow Books.

Rylant, C. 1996. *Henry and Mudge*. New York: Aladdin.

———. 1998. *Tulip Sees America*. New York: Blue Sky Press.

Wilkes, A. 1997. *My First Word Board Book*. New York: Dorling Kindersley.

Wood, A. 1992. *Heckedy Peg*. New York: Voyager.

Young, S. 1994. *Scholastic Rhyming Dictionary*. New York: Scholastic.